JACOBUS ELIZA
JOHANNES CAPITEIN
1717 – 1747

A Critical Study of An

Eighteenth Century African

JACOBUS ELIZA

JOHANNES CAPITEIN

1717 – 1747

A Critical Study of An

Eighteenth Century African

JACOBUS ELIZA JOHANNES CAPITEIN 1717 – 1747

A Critical Study of An
Eighteenth Century African

By
Kwesi Kwaa Prah

SKOTAVILLE

EDUCATIONAL
DIVISION

Published by Skotaville Publishers
(Incorporated Association not for Gain)
307 Hampstead House, 46 Biccard Street
P.O. Box 32483, Braamfontein, 2017

ISBN 0 947009 83 3

Typesetting by Blackshaws (Pty) Ltd. via computer text transfer

Printed and bound by Blackshaws (Pty) Ltd,
Cape Town and Johannesburg

Table of Contents

Introductory Note

I had vaguely known of Capitein before I left Ghana for Europe in 1962. Soon after I arrived in Leiden, I met Dick Wentink, an older student from the Hague, whose studies were being funded by the Hallet Fund. The Hallet Fund had also supported Capitein during the early eighteenth century.

Wentink mentioned Capitein. Kwame Daaku, and later John Fynn, also discussed him with me. But by large, for a long time, I did not pay much attention to Jacobus Eliza Johannes Capitein. However towards the end of my stay in the Netherlands, I developed interest. Increasingly, it dawned on me that possibly I was the first since Capitein to have done a full academic study in that university. The reality was even more poignant, since we were both native to the same corner of Africa. I needed to know more about him. The realisation made me intellectually sympathetic to his history. I drew Willem Wertheim's attention to Capitein, and shortly before I left the Netherlands, he had copied for me Eekhof's study. I collected a few other texts relating to Capitein in Leiden and Amsterdam before I left. Subsequently Simon Simonse helped add to my source material. In Ghana, I often discussed Capitein with Nee Kwate Owoo and Bankie Forster Bankie. We agonized about the black pastor and his infamous defence of slavery. A. J. Prah was a good listener.

I started writing in Cape Coast and completed a rough draft before I left for Southern Africa in 1976, but only looked at it again in Cambridge, in 1980. There I did a last draft. Few additions and subtractions have been made since then.

The art of resurrecting an eighteenth century African is not easy. The danger of his reappearance as an incomplete personality, voiceless and featureless, are for such artistic practitioners too well known. Our Capitein may suffer from some of these inadequacies. But, pitched into the maelstrom of the contemporary trials and tribulations of the African, he may become more fully alive. This has been our objective in this historiographical endeavour. I hope this critical study will assist us Africans, to advance further the process of our mental decolonization, and the struggle for our unity and nationhood.

The Author.

Prospect of the Coast from

A. *Negro* Canoas *carying* Slaves *aboard at* Manfrow

El Mina   S.º *Iago*   Cape Coast

Prospect of S.ᵗ Georges Castle

to Mowri, *from* Barbot & Smith.

Fort Royal *at* Manfrow

Mowri

Mina, *from* Barbot & Dapper.

Conraedsburg *on St.* Jago

Isle de Gomera

Isle de Fer

Isle Canarie

Cap Bojador

Buzadora

TESSET

Lhebichus flu

Ifreng

Guadenum

Albus flu

Tesset

des Caitatis

R. de Or

ZANHAGA

Puteus

Gandia

Futti

Tegassa

C. Bran

ROYAUME DE GUALATA

Angra

Hebedefex

Arguyn

Puteus Arao ou Atza

R. de S. Jean

Woden

C. d'An

Tou de Tabe

Sambaflamec

Cassali

Puteus Araoan

ROYAUME

Porrie

ROYAUME DE TOMBUT

DE GENEHOA

Patefau

Caragoli

Ganar

Kellen

Tocror

Brack

Kockio

Gueguene

R. Senega

Cenehoa

Tombotu

Tombut

PAYS

Cabo Verde

Solcio

Jabu

IALOFES

Budomel

Ioala

Area

Barfola

Nahare

Gambir

Salla

GAMBIA

Gambia

R.

Niger flu

Biafu

Cafamanza

Vintori

Catcheo

Squaxosy R. de Negros

R. Farin

CANTORI

ROYAUME DE

C. Roxo

BIAFARES

Grande

Mandinga

R. S. Domingo

ROYAUME

MANDINGA

Rio Grande

CARAGOLIS

I. de Bijago

DE MELLI

Sousos

Caceres

Punta de Biseye

Ydollos

R. de Sierra Liona

R. Mitomba

Cabo Ledo ou C. Tagrin

MELEGUETTE

I. Massacoy

Flich

Rob Namaya

C. Mo

C. de Mazurad

Sturma

Petit Dieppe

Crou

Gr. Setter

Crowaly

Cabo das Palmas

MER DE

VERD

ERT

cia

olao

Sals

na Vista

Maye

Equateur ou Ligne Equinoctiale

5

10

15

TEGUAT · Cozlo · Sidrama · Yegrad · Techort flu · Techort · Guargala · AGADEMES

Benigdrai · ZIZ · Ghir Flu · TECHORT · GUARGALA

ZUEN ZIGA · Ghir As · Air ou Kenser Desert · Targa et Saora et Zaghara · Lempta ou Suma

Z U E N Z I G A · T A R G A ou

Gooden Desert · Puteus Hair · A Hair · Z A G H A R A · ou L E I · L E M P T

S A A R A · Agaid R Desert · Agades · Digir

ir Desert · Ghir

Agades · Desghir · Germa · Tassaua · Nebrina · PHARANGANA · Ganga · Roy · Secmara

ROYAUME DE AGADES · ROYAUME DE CANO

Mayma · Lac de Gharda · Cano ou Chana · ROYAU DE CASSENA · Cassena

Mura · N E G R E S

Dau · Niger flu · Tirea · Marasa · Nio

Guber · LAMLEN · ROYAUME DE GUBER · Ghanara · Zegzeg · ROY A · Zanfar

DE GAGO · Gago · Acanes Grandes · ROYAUME DE ZEGZEG

Acanes Pequenos · Daum · Daro era · Cosfo · Badis

blanda · Catamanu · Adios · Curano · Benin · ROYAUME DE BENIN

rigom · Camo · Casa de Metina · Gn. Acara · Curams · Ouerrere

Bacorees · Aty · R. de Lagos · R. Cabadaba

Boggu · Atchim · R. de Ramos · del Rey

Laheu · Axim · Corso ou Fort de Nassau · Accra ou Fort de Nassau · Gorgio del Mina · Cabo de 3 Puntas · Cabo Fermosa · Calubg · Facter · Boni · Camarones · R. Borca

GUINÉE · I. Fernando Poo · I. du Prince · Corisco · R. de Antra

ISLE DE S. THOMAS

Cabo de Lopo Gonsalues · Olibata

20 · 25 · 30

Chapter I

A Propos

Harriet Beecher Stowe's portrait of Uncle Tom became during the late 1960s a clear and vivid image of the openly oppressed black who although ruthlessly exploited by Uncle Sam, sought no redress, offered no rebellious resistance like Turner, Vesey, Gabriel or Cato in the cause of his humanity. This type passively accepts his inferior condition, and actively plays the role of a faithful bootlicker of his master. Of course, Stowe did not so intend him. Still today, Uncle Tom represents in social type, the psychologically castrated, politically unconscious, economically underfed, but over-laboured black America. Through centuries of exploitation he had come to be politically benumbed, and psychologically he had fully internalized the myth of the naturalness of his inferior social-economic position. During the last two decades he has been taken out of the fictional world, and made really alive in the characterization of the contradiction between the slavish and reactionary mentality (the "Uncle Tom attitude") on one hand, and the militant or progressive orientation, on the other hand. As such popular condemnations in recent years of Uncle Tom, in fact represent contemporary denunciations of a historically known social phenomenon.

Harriet Beecher Stowe's story today is generally ridiculed for its thick sentimentality and superficial or stereotyped portrayal of blacks. In its own time, it was considered to be powerful propaganda material in the hands of abolitionists and those who in a general sense were sympathetic to the cause of the emancipation of African slaves in America. Some have wrongly suggested that it was one of the causes

1

of the American Civil War, and it has been said of Abraham Lincoln that he once remarked metaphorically to Mrs Stowe that, "So you are the little woman who made this great war". The story *Uncle Tom's Cabin or Life Among the Lowly* was written for serial publication in an abolitionist journal *The National Era*. The book was in its time (1852), a bestseller and was soon variously adapted for the stage. Three newspapers in Paris released it simultaneously. Forty editions of the novel were produced by eighteen publishing houses in Britain. The text was translated over the years into thirty-seven languages, including three Welsh translations.[1]

The African Capitein is a non-fictional figure, however his resemblance to the fictional Uncle Tom is in some respects close. Socially, as a middle class element he was more modestly privileged when compared with Uncle Tom. However, their considerable similarity in the expression of subservient attitudes to exploitative power, under conditions of ruthless national subjugation, cuts them both out of fairly similar archetypal moulds. All the same, it would be pointless and self-defeating for the purposes of the general argument being elucidated in this text, to overstretch and overdraw the similarities between Uncle Tom and Capitein. This is not our aim, for these two figures in many ways, differ substantially. Capitein was not that materialization of docility and tameness which the fictional Uncle Tom was. There is evidence that in his own flabby, inconsequent, and indecisive way, Capitein as time went on, seemed to express inarticulate and rather muted rebellion. This resistance however never fledged fully; remaining an ineffective, essentially defensive posture of a lonely alienated man.

Today the history of Black people is being rewritten. But this exercise is in danger of being hijacked by conservative minds who mythologize about heroes. Like Carlyle such minds would argue ultimately that:

> Universal History, the history of what man has accomplished in this world, is at bottom the history of the Great Men who have worked here. They were the leaders of men, these great ones;

2

the modelers, patterners, and in a wide sense creators, of whatsoever the general mass of men contrived to do or to attain; all things that we see standing accomplished in the world are properly the outer material result, the practical realisation and embodiment, of thoughts that dwelt in the Great Men sent into the world: the soul of the whole world history, it may be considered, were the history of these.[2]

For such thinkers the emphasis in historiography is on leaders and heroes. The masses, the real motor of history are left out. When they are brought into the picture, too often, the mechanism of their social and economic expression, that is, the class struggle is buried under the dung-heap of vulgar hero-mongering. That is not to say that history is not studded with scores of great gems of men who represented the crystallization of the aspirations of the broader masses of the societies in question. Indeed many loosely accepted heroes of African history should be properly appraised in the light of their roles in expressing and reflecting or denying the contemporary wishes of the hoi polloi. The history of Capitein deserves this treatment.

With respect to America, Greenwood in a discussion of Frederick Douglass raises these points very pungently.

> Black revolutionary history, then, is the story of the heroic, unending fight of the black masses to gain complete freedom from the oppressor. It is definitely not the story of a few black men and women who made it into the rapacious capitalist system. It is the story of the masses, the true makers of history. The cunning oppressor has cynically pointed to Negro history and said to the black masses: 'See? Your own history proves that America is truly a land of opportunity. Be good negroes like Booker T. Washington, George Washington Carver, Mary McCleod Bethune, and Marian Anderson and you can make it, too. All you Negroes have to do is work hard, prepare yourselves, obey the law and some day, you too,

will be admitted into the mainstream of the good, old American way of life'. Opportunistic middle-class or petty bourgeois (boozies) Negroes have also co-opted Negro history to act as a wedge to help them force their way into that very same polluted mainstream. The boozies point to Negro history and say: 'See, good white folks? What Negroes have achieved. And I'm like the achievers, not the dirty niggers in the ghetto. Please let me integrate, too.' Both of these attitudes must be exposed and fought, and if the black masses are to advance in our struggle we must now start rejecting 'negro history' and replacing it with 'revolutionary black history', the agonizing, epic story of the black masses' struggle against their captors in America. This story of a nation within a nation must now be told. However, to appraise 'Negro history heroes' critically is to invite the wrath of the black boozies and the frowns of the establishment. But it must be done if we are to move our struggle to a new level. Black revolutionaries must re-examine critically the role our great men and women have played in advancing or retarding the struggle for complete liberation.[3]

That is America, but the situation in most parts of Africa, Asia and Latin America is no different.

Six hundred years ago, Europe and Africa were more or less parallel in the development of productive forces, the material production base for cultural activity were equally, if differently, developed. However, by the mid-18th century at the time of Capitein, European productive forces had advanced far ahead of Africa. Europeans arriving in Africa, were cocksure of themselves and their mores, proud and disdainful of the social existence of the African. Invariably denigratory in their expressed reactions to the African, they were confident in their myths that whatever they thought good must be good, not only for themselves, but for the

4

African. The African could only benefit from their activities and intentions, however dehumanizing this in fact may be, both to themselves and the African. As the Church historian W. Howitt admitted:

> The barbarities and desperate outrages of the so-called Christian race, throughout every region of the world, and upon every people they have been able to subdue, are not to be paralleled by those of any other race, however fierce, however untaught, and however reckless of mercy and shame, in any age of the earth.[4]

They believed their christian culture to be superior to African culture, much more refined, exquisite, purer, more sophisticated than the pagan ecstasies and wild excesses of uncivilised natives. The African should be very satisfied with becoming the ape of his European gods. Building on these myths the European ruling classes could accommodate the 'turning of Africa into a warren for the commercial hunting of black-skins'[5]

A trade which differently destroyed both the exploiter and the exploited. By this time;

> the public opinion of Europe had lost the last remnant of shame and conscience. The nations bragged cynically of every infamy that served them as a means to capitalist accumulation[6]

In Capitein's time as well as today, in many parts of the world, social attitudes of a superior to an inferior class have often been identified with colour. Whites belonged to the superior class and the inferior covered both the free and the enslaved blacks, although it must be admitted that its more emphasized and overt forms were felt most excruciatingly by the slaves, because the depth of their economic bondage was also most clearly defined within the ideological sphere. Culturally it displayed a definiteness of total national subjugation based on class positions of contradiction and struggle within developing capitalist slavocracy. A former slave described an incident experienced in Grenada (1771):

> In April, 1771, I shipped myself as a steward with Capt. Wm. Robertson of the ship *Grenada Planter*, once more to try my fortune in the West Indies; and we sailed from London for Madeira, Barbados, and the Grenadas. When we were at this last place, having some goods to sell, I met once more with my former kind of West India customers. A white man, an islander, bought some goods from me to the amount of some pounds, and made me many fair promises as usual, but without any intention of paying me. He had likewise bought goods from some more of our people, whom he intended to serve in the same manner; but he still amused us with promises. However, when our ship was loaded, and near sailing, this honest buyer discovered no intention or sign of paying for anything he had bought of us; but on the contrary, when I asked him for my money he threatened me and another black man he had bought goods off, so that we found we were likely to get more blows than payment. On this we went to complain to one Mr. McIntosh, a justice of the peace; we told his worship of the man's villainous tricks, and begged that he would be kind enough to see us redressed; but being negroes, although free, we could not get any remedy.[7]

Actually most honest non-European minority group members who have lived or live in Europe today would recognise this type of experience. Indeed an old experience, still fairly regularly met by Africans, Asians, and Latin Americans, in contemporary Europe, not to mention, North America, South Africa, Australia and New Zealand.

Ever since the time of Capitein and before, the European supremacist early or late, has seen the colonized African from the position of a master; the African had to be like the European supremacist wanted to see him. The African lord, peasant, or slave who faithfully reacted and thought as the European nabob wanted was regarded with paternalist affection a known quantity and fairly predictable. He was okay. For the western overlord, the dangerous black was the fellow who fought for his freedom and constantly resisted slavery, chattel or wage. But also till today, when and wherever the African instead of towing the ideological scheme of the dominator, threw down the gauntlet and declared rebellion and resistance, he has been showered with the most heavy downpour of abuse and contemptuous remarks; otherwise as is also frequently the case, with open repressive violence. The rebellious African was not only a physical threat to the oppressor, he was also an ideological threat whose success in resistance created and imposed new realities in fresh light. A situation like this always demanded a reassessment of the structure of the former relations. This process of reappraisal always involved the conscience of the former oppressor; a painful experience although very healthy in the long run. The western supremacist, classical or new, has often been inclined to call the colonized man who vocally and openly resists European cultural and national domination as anti-white in a racialist sense. The colonized man is not expected to protest. So that for example, today in Africa, if and when protest is made even against the presence of some so-called experts, teachers and other Eurocentric economic and cultural agents, one is likely to be described as racialist. This sort of accusation does not always come directly from the westerner, also local indigenous elite elements sing choruses to the tune of their imperial masters.

Capitein's claim to fame or infamy derives from his thesis that slavery is not contrary to Christian principles. Slavery has long been banished from human social intercourse. Capitein continues to be remembered as the African who defended slavery. As Sir Moses Finley has rightly pointed out during the past twenty-five years, the study of slavery,

has reached an intensity without precedent. The

debate has often been bitter, and it has become a public debate, not merely an academic one. It is clear why that should be so; modern slavery was black slavery, and therefore cannot be discussed seriously without impinging on present-day social and racial tensions.[8]

The resurgence of interest in Capitein is also partly due to this current debate and its political undercurrents. Was Capitein such an irredeemable devil's advocate? "How could he betray his roots so thoroughly?" it is often asked. Lobengula in 19th century Southern Africa was tricked into a drunken stupor to "sign" away lands to colonialists. For Lobengula it took alcohol to do the trick, for Capitein was it not the over-kill of a dominant intellectual culture? Are the "black skin white masks" of today seriously different from Capitein?

Capitein's contradictions, the outer manifestations of his inner wranglings loom large when examined today. The absurdities of the period dramatized by the length of the ensuing historical time span and the changes in beliefs, values, and scientifically verified facts of life, present in effect Capitein's weaknesses, in an almost tragico-comic light. However, if, for the sake of argument, the historical specifics of a bygone age are discarded so that the contradictions are stripped of their outer trappings, the mechanism of Capitein's ideological formation becomes something less nebulous, indeed very recognizable, for our own era. Even in such a way that our frequently vulgar westernized antics of the present, dwarf Capitein's, and seem even more distorted and alienated than that 18th century African's.

Today in many parts of Africa, a good proportion of particularly the lower class women, bleach their faces and sometimes other parts of their bodies, in order to have a lighter skin colour. These efforts result in masses of young African women wearing discoloured faces which look like carnival masks (*Kaakamotobi* in Ghana). These women peel off their skins because their equally misguided and confused consorts and husbands compliment their unnatural light-skins. These women generally oppressed within the emergent capitalist and the older precapitalist society respond to the whims of anachronistic male chauvinism. Often the bleaching soap causes sores and other skin diseases for the poor women so anxious to take on a lighter skin. It is not too uncommon on sunny days, to see African women with weeping faces not caused by tears, but by sprawling facial sores. The commonness of skin bleaching indicates the degree to which the idea and association of beauty with white or fair skin is deeply rooted in African society. Regarding this issue, it is interesting to note in passing the African-American experience, Malcolm X referring to his father, wrote that,

> he was subconsciously so afflicted with the white man's brainwashing of Negroes that he inclined to favour the light ones, and I was his lightest child. Most Negro parents in those days would almost instinctively treat any lighter children better than they did the darker ones. It came directly from the slavery tradition that the mulatto, because he was visibly nearer to white, was therefore 'better'.[9]

Throughout the centuries of European domination and exploitation in Africa, the myth of European racial superiority had been fed through the structure of the economic and social systems into the African, to the point that even today it is possible to hear an Ashanti peasant say *Wu yi Nyame a Obroni na eba* (The whiteman is next to God). These days, skin bleaching goes hand-in-hand with wigs, and with this latter sometimes stinking monstrosity to crown the head of a bleached face, African women today are regularly dressed for the carnival of the apes. In much of Africa for certain, before the sixties, wig-wearing was almost unknown, skin bleaching was done but these habits were fairly exceptional. There is evidence that these habits were very much taken on, or better still, borrowed fairly recently from black America. Thus ironically, while within the last two

9

decades African-America was turning Afro, peeling off the muck of Uncle Sam, going natural, and finding their African roots and identity, in their own words "being beautiful"; black Africa, in the expanding shadow of United States global power was picking up cultural props from the U.S. discarded by awakening black America. The *danse macabre* goes on. All this, and more, has resulted in a situation where African boys and girls want to be Afro. What they actually mean is that they want to ape every habit of mind, clothes, or gesture, born in the United States. In the law courts of English-speaking Africa, 18th century wigged "educated" African jurists display, in the name of African justice, the subtleties of Anglo-Saxon law. When these learned gentlemen look in the mirror, they see themselves as "made in Europe". They fail to grasp the fact that this means "made according to the tastes and requirements of imperialism". It is these "made in Europes" of today who when assessing Capitein, often without critical sense, pronounce him heroically, "the first African Protestant educator of the Gold Coast".

In Africa today, few intellectuals, often well trained and versed in the culture and ways of the west, can handle their own indigenous spoken languages with confidence. Most intellectuals can make themselves understood in their mother tongues, but much too often all this is done in a rather superficial, parrot-like fashion. Although they speak their own languages, they cannot write it half as well as they can handle the languages of their former colonial masters. When they speak their mother languages, this is mixed with Europeanising; borrowed words and phrases appear in almost every other sentence, and there are many who quietly believe that the use of European words enhances their prestige in the eyes of their countrymen. All this has gone on today, to such a great extent that many African languages have been prostituted and emasculated beyond all expectation and the threat of slow death is more real than speculative. In this respect, it is striking that Capitein, facing all those social and economic forces during the 18th century, which tended to alienate him from his people, obviously persisted in cherishing his own language so well that he could still handle it sufficiently to translate Euro-Christian passages into Akan. This feat is even more remarkable when one remembers that he left for Europe at a fairly tender age, and after the long sojourn he came back to do translations into Akan which available evidence suggests, was an exercise without precedence in the then Gold Coast.

The ideological subjugation of the African people yesterday and today, is written most clearly in the educational system. From kindergarten through primary, middle and secondary schools, the language of the African child, the only true medium for real and total expression is suppressed. It is made to look and treated as inferior to the language of the former colonial masters. Thus from the early stage, the African child is taught that success in life depends on how close one can get to being Europeanized. Tender age and mental fertility are very impressionable. At the early age the process of developing cultural self-hate in the African is set in steady motion. The middle and secondary schools, created in the image of their European counterparts ensure the glorification of pro-imperialist ideologies dished out in the name of education to the African masses. In the sweltering heat of the African sun, the cultural bondage of the west in Africa, is written on the faces and behaviour of countless upper and lower bureaucrats, who, faithful to the style and manner of the colonial period, consider "proper dressing" to be nothing else but a shirt and tie, preferably an old school tie, plus a jacket to be complete. The whole life-style of the African ruling groups is modelled on Europe and America from the rivers of beer and whisky to African imitations of a British stiff upper lip or a perfect Gallic slur. For the overwhelming majority of African intellectuals today, the structure of their intellectual formation is erected on extreme idealism of a most unsophisticated and vulgar kind, often entailing belief in, and practice of witchcraft, chiliastic christianity, consultation of soothsayers and mallams, and in some occasional instances, a penchant for ritual murder. For these elements of African society, western education has resulted in further confusion, mystification, and bondage of the mind. Westernization remains a veneer of loose habits of mind and body, under which lurks a distorted, culturally split, and subjugated psyche. In African universities today, there is little taught to make the African face himself through an objective examination and understanding of his history in the global human experience. The African universities of today remain firm bastions for breeding alienated elites who in values and orientation, identify more with the western world, than the pauperized masses of Africa, from whose villages and hamlets they originate, and from whom these elites are at the most, often only one or two generations away. This latter fact being the more reason why their alienation from their own roots is so deplorable and tragic. For also, the masses have been ideologically formed to expect their social and economic well-being and independence under the guidance of their educated kinsmen, what Antonio Gramsci has described as 'hegemonic culture'.

The education of the "native races" along western lines was never originally conceived as an end in itself. Although it was often justified by the immediate teachers as such; "the enhancement and betterment of the lesser breeds". Referring to India the historian Macaulay wrote that the aim of the educational policy for the natives was;

> to form a class of interpreters between us and the
> natives we govern, a class of persons Indian in
> blood and colour but English in tastes, in
> opinions, in morals and in intellect.[10]

It was an educational or socialization process which on the one hand universalized scientific and logical approaches to the native's understanding of nature, but also enslaved the native to his master's tastes, voice, and ideas; too often in a superficial fashion, leaving the native mesmerized, in confusion, and a sort of "cultural schizophrenia". The African through such education is then enslaved by the myth of the process of wanting to free and better oneself by becoming what one is not. When truth or facts are robbed of their natural setting or context, they become lies.

The African experience to date has been largely documented by westerners. The African has been recorded through western eyes and has through his education learnt to see himself as others see him. The self is perceived from the outside, but this has generally not been balanced against a view from inside. Also specifically, the outsider has not and is still not a disinterested party. Rather the westerner has historically been the economic and cultural rapist of the African and too often western perspectives of the African experience have surreptitiously justified without questions, the role of the West in Africa. The true conscience of the West in Africa, like Sir Roger Casement, André Gide, E.D. Morel, Basil Davidson, Lord Brockway or Michael Scott, are generally regarded by the rest of western observers as marginal men, who are freaks in the sense of being extraordinarily removed from the mainstream of dominant opinion. Unfortunately the lower and less informed classes in the West are taught by their more affluent kinsmen through their control of institutions of education, information, and media; and are too often stimulated and mentally bred with subtle chauvinism and disguised jingoism. The African factually knows more about the history of the West than his own; and the educated African is often at pains to display to all, how well-versed he is in the history, culture, and the ways of the West. Taught to see himself through the eyes of the other, the westernized native is often without full cognisance, ashamed of himself and his history as he knows it. He becomes an inveterate escapist, constantly running away from his being, in his attempt to be like the other; and the more he tries to live in the surrealistic world of the absurd, the world and history which does not belong to him, the more he invites the contempt and abuse of his western bondsmen. Perhaps an example of this breed would be Dillibe Onyeame, a Nigerian upper middle class element who was schooled at the elite English school, Eton. The effect on this intelligent African was traumatic, as he later recounts and regurgitates in his *John Bull's Nigger* and *Nigger at Eton*. He indulges in excesses of eloquent, keen, but pitiless self-flagellation. The reader of Onyeame cannot help understanding that the author is deeply wounded and ashamed of his origins without him really realizing it. This is what the effects of exclusive British education did to its first African ward.

Du Bois' words from 1919 ring too true for dispute.

> The methods by which this continent has been stolen have been contemptible and dishonest beyond expression. Lying treaties, rivers of rum, murder, assassination, mutilation, rape, and torture have marked the progress of the Englishman, German, Frenchman, and Belgian on the Dark Continent. The only way in which the world has been able to endure the horrible tale is by deliberately stopping its ears and changing the subject of conversation while the devilry went on.[11]

However, much certain minds would try to play down the facts, one fact stares us all resolutely and constantly in the face, and this is that; throughout the 500 odd years of Euro-African relations, a very dominant ideological feature of this connection, has been the racism of the West towards Africans and people of African descent; be it in Africa, Europe, the West Indies, or the Americas. As I write these words, right here in the continent of Africa, in the land of their fathers and forefathers, Africans are kept under the jackboot of unrelenting white racist minorities. Under these conditions, the treachery of other Africans intent on maintaining unqualified dialogue with these white racists is appalling, for it stands against the tide of history and the just and noble aspirations of the African people.

It is easy for obscurantist thinkers to vulgarize or attempt to blunt the edge of our argument by consciously or false-consciously misconstruing our points and strictures. Condemnation of the West for the evil-reeking atrocities it has perpetrated in all parts of the non-western world, not to mention the social crimes at home is definitely not intended as a reactionary chauvinist stance of actually misguided nationalism on our part.

Scientific objectivity cannot mean the denial by deafening silence the true record of oppressed people, and it is only human and realistic to be emotional about facts and realities which are truly moving in their cruel and inhuman impact. It is part of the conditions of the civilized mind to raise an aware and moral voice in righteous indignation; to push the pen more furiously and sensitively to historical records which define our universal humanity or inhumanity. When we do this, we are not simply moralizing and condemning evils. More than that as Herbert Aptheker has written it is; "because struggling against them educates and unites people".[12]

What position does one take to the western record in Africa? We are certainly not suggesting that everything that has happened to Africa as a result of Western expansion into African has been deplorable and in effect negative; that all Africans are innocent angels and all Westerners devils. Such crude views are not unfamiliar but they are as distorted and warped as the ideas of the Eurocentrists and Western racists.

Our view-point shares a common platform with Marx, who in his piece on *The Effects of British Rule in India*, indicated that,

> England, it is true, in causing a social revolution in Hindustan, was actuated only by the vilest interests, and was stupid in her manner of enforcing them. But that is not the question. The question is, can mankind fulfil its destiny without a fundamental revolution in the social state of Asia? If not, whatever may have been the crimes of England, she was the unconscious tool of history in bringing about that revolution.

Thus the expansion of the West was in effect a double-edged sword cutting differently on opposite sides. On the one hand it was atrociously exploitative and destructive for all the precapitalist peoples capitalism sought to control. On the other hand, it introduced new and more historically advanced forces and relations of production while bringing under its growing capitalist control, the means of production. Historically more advanced forces and relations of production in their development, correspond to the development of social classes, so that the expansion of one develops coterminously with the other. The new emergent classes express the consciousness of their material positions in the relations of production. In this whole exercise, to inject here Mason's honest remarks,

> At first the native is often puzzled, particularly in Africa and particularly by the missionaries. Here, for instance, are very rich people, with far more possessions than he has seen before — hatchets, guns, chairs, tables — and clearly obsessed with property, anxious for land on which to build houses bigger than any he has seen before — and yet they preach to him about taking no more thought for the morrow than the ravens and the lilies of the field.... But, on the whole, puzzled and often critical though he may be, the native accepts the European's self-confidence, his technical skill, his success, as signs that he has something that is worth acquiring. He accepts the European's valuation of his own society, starts to learn in a missionary school, and absorbs the symbolism of Blake's poem. He accepts a position in the hierarchy of inequality. His soul is white already and his actions will grow whiter until, like Blake's little boy, he is free from the grime of his body; and then, as in the poem, the two will play together side by side.[13]

This is the stuff of which the Capiteins were made. In a sense, as we shall see, Capitein is Caliban and his Dutch mentors Prospero. Some years ago Mannoni saw what use Shakespeare's creation in fact can be put, to elucidate the psychology of the colonizer and the colonized.[14] The West India Company created Capitein but he never became what they had in all respects hoped he would be. Like Caliban he could have said,

"You taught me language, and my profit on't is, I know how to curse".

Notes

CHAPTER I

1. S. Everett. *The Slaves*. New York, 1978, p 164.
2. T. Carlyle. *On Heroes, Hero-worship and the Heroic in History*. 5th May 1840.
3. Frank G. Greenwood: Frederick Douglass and U.S. Imperialism *Monthly Review*. April. 1973. pp. 42 and 43.
4. William Howitt. *Colonization and Christianity*. A Popular History of the Treatment of the Natives by The Europeans in all their Colonies. London. 1838. p. 9.
5. K. Marx. Ibid.
6. K. Marx. Ibid.
7. Paul Edwards. (ed.). *Equiano's Travels*. London. 1967. 1969 Edition. pp. 128-129.
8. M. Finley. *Ancient Slavery and Modern Ideology*. London. 1980 Preface.
9. Malcolm X. *Autobiography*. Harmondsworth. 1965. pp. 82-83.
10. Quoted here from James Morris. *Pax Brittanica*. Harmondsworth 1979. p. 140.
11. W.E.B. Du Bois. African Roots of War. *Monthly Review*. April, 1973.
12. H. Aptheker: *The Negro People in America. A Critique of G. Myrdal's An American Dilemma*. New York. 1946. p 31.
13. Philip Mason ... but O'. My Soul is White, *Encounter Magazine*. April. 1968. p. 59. It is perhaps worth noting that actually Capitein's friend. Brandijn Ryser, has verse in praise of Capitein, which when translated comes very close to Mason's text quoted here. On page 157, footnote 1, sub (a) of the 4th edition of Capitein's thesis, Brandijn Ryser has the following lines on Capitein: "De schijn bedriegt: waarom? dit zwart doch zeedig wezen, Bekleet de blanke ziel van d'Africaanschen Moor", loosely translated reads as follows: "The appearance deceives: why? this black but demure being contains the white soul of the African moor".The whole poem appears also in Eekhof's study, page 22.The poem appears also in German (Hoogduitse) and is reproduced in the *Navorscher* (1855).
14. O. Mannoni. *Prospero and Caliban*. New York. 1964.

Chapter II

Bibliographical Considerata

The uniqueness of Capitein's historical role has attracted some attention in the past; especially during the first hundred and fifty years following his death. It is, however, no exaggeration to say that, in the light of his significance to African history, it is a surprise that particularly in Africa, it has not generated as much discussion as one would have wished or expected. Till today, indeed, little factual knowledge about the man and his times is circulating even in Ghana. Instead, a vague sort of nationalist hero-mongering based often on the scantiest of information is what one invariably comes across among Africans when Capitein is mentioned or discussed.

Nationalism or African self-assertiveness, useful and important as it has been, has also for many Africans, been often more resoundingly, without sufficient intellectual ballast. Among many, it has created a narrowly populist perspective, thoroughly inward-looking in structure, often apt to unscientifically glorify periods and personages in African history, and more often quite chauvinist in outlook. All the same, to deny or distort the social significance of nationalism would be intellectually irresponsible, since, till today in the context of the African revolution, in some areas and particularly within certain spheres of the struggle for national liberation, the nationalist position represents the leading position.

A cursory examination of what has been written on

Capitein reveals the class and historical basis of most of the prejudices which have been put into print about him from the earliest times. These writings variously represent the thinking and interests of the western ruling classes vis a vis the "phenomenon" Capitein through the corresponding historical stages of capitalist development. The distance in years between Capitein and us of the present or the near future, plus more careful examination of historical evidence has exposed the rougher crudities of the older commentators. Indeed, the most diligent and conscientious of Capitein's biographers has written that,

> When one reads these things, one asks oneself, who is to blame: the poor negro, on whom such falsehoods and unprovable accusations are attributed; or those who carry on such incorrect methods of historical enquiry and historical writings?[1]

Technical limitations such as simple carelessness and misinformation could take part of the blame. Indeed, few authors are always immune to this disease. However, the essentials of the mystification are much more fundamentally grounded. They derive from the very nature of bourgeois historiography, which presents its ideology as history, and which can be unravelled only by a critical reference and examination of the historical realities which bourgeois science continuously emasculates and deforms. Thus, it is the analysis of these ideologies which opens the way to a more scientifically structured and systematically critical perspective of history. This exercise, in fact, enables us to grasp the nature of ideology as a class-bound phenomenon, so that we understand ideologies as indeed typical of historical epochs and representing corresponding forms of consciousness, which cannot be understood unless they are fully related to the contemporary modes of production and exchange. We are not suggesting here an over-determination which makes man a mere and total tool of forces beyond his control and on which he has no influence.

Some social scientists maintain that ideology is a monopoly of the left, that ideology is historical materialism, the intellectual *bête noire* of western philosophy; that they, on the other hand, espouse a value-free science which has no ideological class content. They fail to comprehend that, in a sense, when understood as a *weltanschauung*, a world outlook, every individual has a view, a way of perceiving and interpreting the realities in which men live. This outlook, is nothing else but the frame of reference created and conditioned by the historical material conditions through which the socialization and the whole maturation process of that person takes place. Thus, all men have their own ideologies depending largely on their class origins and contemporary social class positions, or a conscious reaction to these factors. So that even the idea that they do not have ideological positions is in itself an ideological standpoint.

The earliest bibliographical material of interest are to be found in the first and fourth editions of the Dutch translated versions of his thesis. In both of these editions, seven praise poems written in honour of Capitein are to be found, though these poems do not offer any real information about Capitein's life and work.[2] They represent, indeed, the excited response of Dutch contemporaries to the uniqueness, the exotic character of Capitein; an African primitive who has been "civilized", was for these minds, an object of exhibition; a subject beyond reality, a freak, but real enough to speak to those large audiences his sermons and talks attracted. However, fortunately, there exists considerable tit-bits of concrete information, notes and remarks on Capitein, sprinkled through a few European, mainly Dutch and German journals of church history, published since the 18th century. Out of these scattered points of information, A. Eekhof[3] has pieced together the only full blown study on Capitein published during the second decade of this century. In fact, also Eekhof's study was originally published in the *Dutch Archival Journal for Church History*. Subsequently in 1917, it was released as a single study. Eekhof threw some factual light on some areas of darkness about Capitein's life history. He debunked distortions and false reports which several 19th century writers had manufactured or passed on. The 1742 to 1747 period, when Capitein operated as a pastor in the *St. George D'Elmina* has particularly been given a lavish paint of fantasy. Ijpeij and Dermout, (*Geschiedenis Der Nederlandsche Hervormde Kerk*) after reviewing the history of missionary work in Asia went on to say that during the early 18th century successes particularly in Batavia gave hope to the aspiration that,

> the Reformed Church through Dutch influence could agreeably expand into Africa. But the hope was unfortunately smothered with great sadness for the Dutch Reformed Church. It is known that, on the coast of Guinea, in the Ethiopian Sea, at the port and post of St. George D'Elmina, which then as now belonged to the Netherlands; there was a Reformed parish. It was expected that perhaps through the efforts of the leaders of the community, in the interest of the expansion of Christianity it may be possible to spread the mission among the local heathens. Things however turned out differently than was hoped. A Guinean moor of about eight was sold in 1725 to a Dutch sea-captain. The latter gave the African youngster as a gift to a Dutch trader of the Directors of the East India Company, who took him to the Hague, where he was taught the Dutch language and writing. He was also educated and brought up as a Christian and baptised as Jakob Eliza Johannes Capitein. He was so strongly evangelized that he chose theology as study and plunged whole-heartedly into it. He was for this reason given a classical Latin education and sent to Leyden University, to be trained for public service. Here, again this promising youngster acquitted himself well, and under the supervision of Prof. Van Den Honert defended a dissertation in Latin. In 1742 he passed his Church examinations and was despatched as pastor to

D'Elmina. This is about all one knows with respect to his work. Once in Elmina he defected to his blood-relations, among whom perhaps his parents still were. He traced them and was weak enough to allow himself to betray Christianity which he had appeared to have firmly internalized, and again became a heathen. It was rumoured from D'Elmina that soon after his arrival there he went inland and disappeared among his people.[4]

These writers were suggesting that, in fact, Christian culture had been a thin decorative coating protecting the thick skin of a veritable barbarian. In an earlier study written by Ijpeij[5] and published in 1797, he had presented the same points on Capitein as is set out in his joint study with Dermout in 1824. However, in the earlier work Ijpeij is mildly cynical about members of the Christian Dutch public in whose living rooms one finds sometimes displayed, copper-print engravings of Capitein's portrait. Ijpeij pointed out to the Dutch public what he considered to be the "completely incurable blindness of some heathens".[6] Was this not actually the use of religious belief and ethnic bias to quietly and implicitly assert European superiority? This notion of the tendency for westernized natives to fall back into their "primitive" religious habits when in a crisis or re-exposed to their traditional religious culture was especially in the 18th and 19th centuries a recurring view of westerners about natives they had educated. Capitein was not the first, neither was he the last. This was the era of heavy Atlantic slave traffic, which brought prosperity to the propertied classes in Europe. The economic gains of expanding European capitalism had to be maintained, and so long as religious historians and other intellectuals could juggle involved arguments to prove the inferiority and subhuman nature of the African, there was nothing wrong with buying and selling blacks. A.J. van der Aa also substituted colourful imagination for historical facts. It seems most of Van der Aa's material on Capitein is drawn from Ijpeij's earlier study. Indeed most of it is a direct reproduction of Ijpeij. He however makes his own fresh additions to the distortions of Capitein's history by adding that after Capitein had gone inland to his people and betrayed Christianity,

> It is possible that he died en route or possibly, was murdered by his tribesmen.[7]

Van der Aa however has an extensive bibliography on the work of Capitein.[8]

By and large, by the beginning of the 19th century the story that Capitein on his return to Elmina, turned-coat on the Church and became a heathen had gained the status of fact in the minds of most people who knew anything about him. Perhaps more than anybody Ijpeij had been responsible for the spread of this fable in the Netherlands through his publication of 1797. Ijpeij distortions were especially unfortunate since his high academic credentials must have given his work great but unfortunately misplaced respectability. He had been a member of the Zeeland Society of Science (*Zeeuwsche Genootschap der Wetenschappen*) in Vlissingen, and pastor at Etten. Later he obtained a doctorate degree and became Professor of Theology in the University of Groningen. His collaborator Dermout was also well placed, as Secretary of the General Synod of the Dutch Reformed Church and pastor in the Hague. Between them certainly a more careful approach to their work would have been expected. Most of Capitein's 19th century biographers drew their material from Ijpeij and Dermout.[9] Capitein is referred to in the *Christelijk Maandschrift* (1854).[10] In the *Beknopt Biographisch Handwoordenboek Van Nederland* (1854) edited by Kobus and De Rivecourt, we are told that while in Holland, Capitein's mentors had formed the impression that as a missionary he would be especially suitable for evangelical work among his compatriots.

This would suggest further that his career selection was not an altogether autonomous choice. Regarding his life in Elmina, Kobus and De Rivecourt repeat Ijpeij's story but give it an even more exaggerated and dramatic twist. They wrote that,

> as soon as he landed he looked up his
> consanguines and instead of preaching the gospel,
> he dropped Christianity and became again a
> heathen.

Rumours and stories always have a way of enriching
themselves through more distortions as the rumours become
more rampant. Capitein is also written about in Van
Abkoude's *Naam lijst van Nederduitsch Boeken*. During the second
half of the 19th century, the *Navorscher* published a number of
researches on the life and times of Capitein.[11] It was largely
through the researches appearing in this journal that the
most serious and systematic attempts were initiated in the
effort to gain a more precise and historically faithful picture
of our man. Data relating to his life in the Netherlands was
generally easy to find and was precise. There were few points
of contradiction and these were of fairly unimportant
character. What remained still ambiguous and unclarified
were the reports dating from the 18th century relating to his
life in Elmina. Probably one could safely say that the
definitive beginnings of a proper correction to the older
stories appeared in the *Navorscher* of 1877. In one of the
issues of the journal for that year, L. Proes who was brother-
in-law of Lieutenant-Col. C.J.M. Nagtglas, who had been the
Dutch governor in Elmina responsible for the Dutch
possessions on the West Coast of Africa, stated that his
brother-in-law had in about 1860 sent him some data taken
out of archives of the West India Company at *St. George
D'Elmina*. The material which is presented adds considerably
to giving us some clues as to Capitein's fortunes or
misfortunes during the final years of his life. They relate
particularly to heavy debts incurred by Capitein during this
period.[12] L. Proes reports also that Nagtglas informed him
that;

> I could not find anything relating to his death.
> The archive has suffered greatly from the climate,
> and there is a lot which is indecipherable. His

25

undertaking to pay off his debts were probably never honoured.[13]

Subsequently after reading an article by Muller on Capitein, Proes had again consulted his in-law, long after his tenure as Governor. Nagtglas' answer had been that,

> I imagine that the debts which Capitein fell into at Elmina quickly put him in an untenable position, and made him lose his standing in the eyes of the community, and this made it possible for him to be lured into fetishism and disappear into heathenism. My register for Dutch pastors is incomplete with respect to a number of years, among which are the years Capitein was supposed to have served as pastor. In 1764, Gerardus Verbeet became pastor in Elmina. Could the archives of that period not provide any information?[14]

Nagtglas then actually referred his in-law to Ijpeij and Dermout, for the final word. In the same year, 1877, another writer signing himself as *Laboranter* pulled a coup in the whole story. Writing in the *Navorscher* he confidently said,

> I can assure Mr. Proes that the pastor Capitein in Elmina did not fall back into fetishism, neither did he disappear. He died in Elmina on the 1st February 1747. This information can be found in a letter from the Director-General of the Guinea Coast dated 1st April 1747 addressed to the Presidential Committee of the Zeeland Chamber of the West India Company. This letter contains apart from an explanation for the charges made by the pastor Capitein to the Directors of the West India Company about the shoddy behaviour of some of the employees of the company; also some information from which, among other things, one gets the impression that his apparent inclination towards commerce was probably one of the reasons for his debts.[15]

26

Thus in 1877 the major question marks about Capitein's life were largely removed. Silvanus' paper on Capitein which appeared in A.W. Bronsveld's *Stemmen Voor Waarheid and Vrede*,[16] was published in the last decade of the 19th century and took account of the corrections which the *Laboranter's* diligent work had brought to light. Silvanus' piece however lacked the polish and perhaps sympathy for his subject which was displayed two decades later by Capitein's first important 20th century biographer Eekhof.

Eekhof's study of 1916, also exposed the extravagant distortions of the earlier writers. Some of the very early writers, Ernst Ludewig Rathlef and J.C. Strodmann,[17] did not indulge in dishing out the sort of misinformation which later writers provided in their tastelessly over-spiced historiographical concoctions. Eekhof indicates in his study hitherto unknown sources of information on Capitein and makes altogether the best study so far done on Jacobus Eliza Johannes Capitein, the first black slave who was ordained minister in Europe (the Netherlands), 20 years before his better known countryman, Philip Quacoe. Capitein features in the famous Gold Coast nationalist S.R.B. Attoh-Ahuma's work *Memoirs of West African Celebrities* (1905). This work is an edited collection of brief biographies of various historical figures from West African history. Most of these studies are taken from various other authors; Attoh-Ahuma tells us that the object of his collection is;

> to the serious study of *the rising generation* who, ignorant of the intellectual traditions and prestige of our beloved country, have not seen the footprints of our great men on the sands of time; and do but faintly hear their distant footsteps echo through the corridors of time. These brief memoirs are loyally and most affectionately commended.[18]

The piece on Capitein is by the Abbé Henri-Baptiste Gregoire (1750-1831), Bishop of Blois.[19] Gregoire became an advocate for the recognition of African humanity. His best known work attempted to demonstrate that Africans are intellectually and morally not inferior to Europeans. In this effort Gregoire set himself against the arguments of writers like David Hume and Edward Long.[20] The Abbé's efforts earned him the sobriquet,

"the new Las Casas", "defender of the cause of liberty and unfortunate people",[21]

With regard to Capitein's defence of slavery, the Abbé Gregoire shares clearly the view expressed by Silvanus that the poor man was pressurized to make that case. His words are that:

The Dutch planters, persuaded that slavery is inconsistent with Christianity, but stifling the voice of conscience, probably instigated Capitein to become the apologist of a bad cause ...[22]

Gregoire's sympathetic and liberal approach to his subject has also in other ways been historically vindicated. He takes up the matter of the rumours which ran round about Capitein's life in Elmina and his defection to heathenism thus:

In 1802 a vague report was spread that he had abjured Christianity and embraced idolatry again. Blumenbach however who inserted a portrait of Capitein in his work on the varieties of the human race, could detect no authentic information against him.[23]

Attoh-Ahuma also reacts strongly to the contemporary falsehoods of Capitein's story as it was then known to be. In the introduction to his text he draws parallels between Capitein and Philip Quacoe:

There is food for reflection in the fact that to Capitein was given the foremost place in the vanguard of Christian propagandism to the men of Guinea. He was, as far as we know, the first native missionary Europe sent out to minister to the spiritual necessities of his compatriots. We must not forget the arduous and self-denying labours of Philip Quacoe, who for 50 years filled with conspicuous success the position of Colonial Chaplain at Cape Coast Castle. Capitein, however, was Quacoe's senior in the mission field; for years previously, he had begun to hold forth the word of life to the people of Elmina. We pass over, with the contempt it deserves, the vile insinuation that was current years ago as to Capitein's ultimate apostasy. Curiously enough the same unfounded charge was in later years preferred against the fragrant memory of pious Philip Quacoe. With regard to the former, Blumenbach exposed the falsity of the scandal, and proved it to be without foundation.[24]

It was Johann Friedrich Blumenbach (1752-1840) from whom Gregoire drew his evidence on Capitein. In various writings published towards the end of the 18th century and the early part of the 19th century, Blumenbach sought scientifically to establish that there are five different races of men who together share the unity of humankind.[25] Capitein's portrait features as a prototype of the negro. As to the significance of Blumenbach's work, Marx was one of the first to have recognized its importance. In a memorial lecture he presented to the Royal Society of Science on the 8th February 1840, he drew attention to the fact that:

At the time when negroes and the savages were still considered as half animals, and no one had yet conceived the idea of the emancipation of the slaves, Blumenbach raised his voice, and showed that their physical qualities were not inferior to those of the Europeans, that even amongst the latter themselves the greatest possible differences existed, and that opportunity alone was wanting for the development of their higher faculties.[26]

29

Like all the previous biographers of Capitein, Blumenbach was also piqued by Capitein's Elmina history. He observed that:

> according to the circumstances there are two stories about his fate (at D'Elmina); either namely that he was murdered or that he went back to his own savage countrymen, and exchanged their superstitions and mode of life for what he had learnt in Europe. In this last case, his history forms a pendent to that of the Hottentot who was brought up in Europe and civilized, whose similar and thorough patriotism has been immortalized by Rousseau (in his *Discourse sur L'inégalite parmi les hommes*).[27]

Blumenbach showed in comparison to the other biographers, stronger scientific vein by indicating that with respect to the various rumours and versions as to Capitein's eventual fate in Elmina, he could detect no authentic information against him. Attoh-Ahuma reacted strongly to the tendency for westerners who all too quickly on the weakest and scantiest of evidence, suggest that Africans who have been ostensibly trained and cultured in the tradition of the west defect to their primitive origins, sooner or later, once they are back within their original cultural milieu. On this score, in the appendix to his book, he took Viscount Wolseley to task. In the latter's *Story of a Soldier's Life*, he wrote that:

> At Cape Coast Castle we all attended divine service every Sunday. The Colonial Chaplain who ministered there was the very blackest of Negroes, but had received a university education in England. His salary was nearly 600 pounds a year, and beyond reading the service to about thirty people on Sundays, he did nothing. The episcopal schools were a public disgrace, and . for their condition he was directly responsible. I remember

hearing years afterwards, but I cannot vouch for the story, that when he was dying he sent for the chief fetish man of the town saying he preferred his ministrations, in which he had faith, to the consolation of the Christian religion in which he did not believe. So much for our educated West Coast of Africa converts.

Attoh-Ahuma's reaction was sharp and pointed. After arguing that Wolseley is held in great esteem on the Gold Coast he scathingly remarked:

When therefore, under the shadow of a great name, the Field Marshall lends himself to the perpetuation of a tale for which he could not vouch, when he presses into service his unique personality in the circulation of what on the face of it is absolutely mendacious, he sets us a problem in psychology not at all easy of solution.[28]

The historical repetition and persistence of such stories obviously bothered Attoh-Ahuma greatly. He was prepared to be skeptical enough to say that:

Where there is smoke, proverbial presumption assures us, there must be fire of some sort, and we may well enquire into the origin of this well-worn story of clerical relapse into idolatry, which for three consecutive centuries have been used in the art of mud-throwing at more than two African clergymen, and with which some have dared to soil the sunbeams of blameless lives; and one author at least, has given articulation and expression to it in his *Strange Stories*.[29]

Attoh-Ahuma then reminds us that the veteran Basel Lutheran Mission minister Rev. Carl Reindorf writing about Capitein's historical successor Philip Quacoe noted that:

He was declared to have relapsed into idolatry, as
some charms or fetishes were found under his
dying pillows and bed ... even if such were the
case, we are quite certain they were not placed
there by himself, or by his orders, for it is a fact
that, not only the native Christians, but even
Europeans as well, have often been thus treated
by their heathen friends attending them as nurse
or doctor.[30]

Attoh-Ahuma then goes on to draw our attention to the
fact that the same insinuations were made against Capitein's
memory; but that after investigations into the matter,
Blumenbach,

was able to prove to the hilt that he was not guilty
of any such apostasy.[31]

Bartels has also produced a brief and neat study of
Capitein. He pays particular attention to the educational-
historical aspects of his subject, but offers no critical and
analytical insight into the subject.[32] In a recent book by I.S.
Ephson, a short piquant biographical sketch of Capitein is
included.[33] This last is, perhaps, the poorest study so far
made of Capitein, to the knowledge of the present author.

The above-mentioned writers and commentators on
Capitein are technically similar in one fundamental sense
although to different degrees. None of them has a critical
materialist approach; none of them examines Capitein in a
truly historical and dialectical way, so that his class position
within the contemporary class structure, both of Elmina and
the Netherlands of his time, is woefully neglected. Instead,
Capitein is discussed in an eclectic and ahistorical fashion.
We are not made to understand why Capitein behaved and
believed those social expressions he historically manifested.
The result perhaps is that his true meaning in history is
generally misplaced. It is probably useful to point out that, if
history is written in such a way that individuals are treated
as islands, that is, that those historical figures are not placed

in their socio-economic milieu, so that the contradictions arising out of the contemporary class struggles are mirrored in the specific figures in question, then the whole scientific exercise falls into undefined and unchartered waters, in which sentiments, loose and materially unfounded statements, are presented as facts.

Men make their own histories, their successes, and failures. They make their decisions according to options as they appear to them in a given period and on the basis of their internalized values. Even the available options result from possibilities created and endorsed by history and are meaningful only when considered in connection with the historical conditions crystallized and represented in the personalities. Simple minds are apt to dwell unnecessarily on kings and so-called heroes or leaders. But leaders are leaders of men, interests, and the forces of history. Under no circumstances are men free from the conditions of their social existence. Men have inclinations and character traits, that is, psychological formations which set them uniquely apart from others. However, their unique personalities are not conditioned and formed from nowhere. Rather, they are formed by the correlations and intercorrelations of the social material forces of history, and even the most apparently insignificant habit of mind or action, cannot be really grasped without a fundamental understanding of the essentials of the material processes of history within the culture or society in which our individual was formed and plays his "unique" role. His uniqueness does not deny his universality. Neither does his universal qualities which are historically and materially developed exclude all characterization specifying his particularity. Rather these aspects of the human phenomenon dialectically relate, totalize, and define our man. He created history in as much as history created him.

Notes

CHAPTER II

1. A. Eekhof. *De Negerpredikant*. 1916. p. 5.
2. The list of these poems are documented in Eekhof's study. p. 23. See Below. Mention should also be made of Brandijn Ryser's poem on Capitein which appeared on F. Van Bleiswijcks' engraved portrait of Capitein published by Phillipus Bonk. (Mentioned in footnote 13 of Chapter I in this text).
3. A. Eekhof. Op Cit. *De Negerpredikant, Jacobus Elisa Joannes Capitein : Bijdrage tot de kennis van onze kolonial Kerkgeschiedenis. Nederlandsch Archief voor Kerkgeschiedenis*. Deel XIII. Den Haag. 1916. Most of the material in this paper especially in the bibliographical aspects are drawn from the above named text.
4. A. Ijpeij and I.J. Dermout. *Geschiedenis der Nederlandsche Hervormde Kerk*. Breda. 1824. Deel III. pp. 401-403. See my reference from Bosman to Lewis Hannibal in the last chapter of this present study.
5. A. Ijpeij. *Geschiedenis van de Kristilijk Kerk in de achttiende eeuw*. Utrecht. 1779. Deel I. Stuk I. p 64.
6. A. Ijpeij. Ibid.
7. A.J. Van der Aa. *Biographisch Woordenboek*. Haarlem, 1858. Deel III. pp. 171-172.
8. A.J. Van der Aa. Ibid.
9. Some of the researchers and biographers are only mentioned with initials: H.J.S: C.W. Bruinvis: J.C.K. and F.M.See *Navorscher* 1855. The authors add that in a collection of Portraits of Famous Theologians (*Portretten van beroemde Godgeleerden*), published by Soetens and Sons, in The Hague,a portrait of Capitein is included.
10. *Christelijk Maandschrift*. 1854. p. 419.
11. One of the 1877 issues summarises the references concerned under. Asar XXVI. p. 611. XXVII. p. 49, followed by IV. p 262; V. p. 90 and supplement 1855. pp. 71, 72, 146. See *Navorscher* 1877. p. 11 where the above are listed.
12. *Navorscher* 1877. pp. 49-51.
13. *Navorscher*. Ibid. p. 51.
14. *Navorscher*. Ibid. p. 52.
15. *Navorscher*. Ibid. p. 155.
16. A.W. Bronsveld (ed) *Stemmen voor Waarheid en Vrede*,Utrecht. 1891. pp. 1085-1100.
17. Ernst Ludewig Rathlef. *Geschichte Jeztlebenden Gelehrten, als eine Fortsetzung des Jeztlebenden Gelehrten Europa*. 1743.
18. S.R.B. Attoh-Ahuma. *Memoirs of West African Celebrities*. Liverpool. 1905. Opening to the collection.
19. Henri Gregoire. *De la Littérature des Négres, on Recherches sur leur facultes intellectuelles, leur qualités morales, et leur littérature; suivies de notices sur la vie et les ouvrages des Négres qui si sont distingués dans les science, les lettres et les arts*. Paris. 1808.

20. David Hume. Of National Characters. In T.H. Green and T.H. Grose (ed) *Essays. Moral, Political, and Literary*. London. 1975. Edward Long. *The History of Jamaica; or a General Survey of the Ancient Modern State of that Island with Reflections on its Situation, Settlements, Inhabitants, Climate, Products, Commerce, Laws, and Government*. (3 vols). London. 1774. The debate is discussed with considerable elaborateness by Henry L. Gates. *The History and Theory of Afro-American Literary Criticism (1773-1831). The Arts, Aesthetic Theory, and Nature of the African*. Ph.D. Thesis. University of Cambridge. 1978. See also J. Gardner. *History of Jamaica*. London, 1876. pp. 207-208.

21. Julian Prevost, Comte de Limonade, Letter to the Abbé Gregoire, June 10, 1814, Arsenal 6399, Folio 44-47.Fr. de Tussac (*Cri des colons contre un ouvrage de M. l'éuêque et a Sénateur Gregoire, ayant pour titre de la litterature des négres, ou réfutation des inculpations calomnieuses faites aux Colons par l'auteur, et par les autres philosophes negrophiles, tels que Raynal, Valmont,de Bomare, etc*. Paris. 1810) attacks Gregoire's arguments basically on the grounds that real Africans have nothing in common with the examples of western trained Africans who the Abbé uses to make his case i.e. examples like Capitein, Amo, Juan Latino, are not really representative African cultural products. (See H.L. Gates op.cit).

22. Quoted here from S.R.B. Attoh-Ahuma. Op. Cit. p. 22.

23. Abbé Gregoire. Ibid. Quoted from Attoh-Ahuma. p. 20.

24. 9 Attoh-Ahuma. Ibid. Introduction.

25. Perhaps Blumenbach's principal works in this respect are his: (a) *Beytrage zur Naturgeschichte*. Gottingen. 1790 and 1806. (b) *Uber die naturlichen Verschiedenheiten im Menschengeschlecht*. Leipzig. 1798.

26. K. Marx. *Zum andenken an Johann Friedrich Blumenbach.Eine Gedactniss-Rede Gehalten in der Sitzung der Koniglicken Societat der Wissenschaften den 8 Feb. 1840*.Gottingen. 1840.

27. Blumenbach. *Beytrage zur Natuurgeschichte*. Quoted here from H.L. Gates. Op cit. Vol 2. p. 380.

28. S.R.B. Attoh-Ahuma. Ibid. p. 241. Attoh-Ahuma was able to trace, identify as still living, the Colonial Chaplain in question. In the last paragraph he wrote that: "The age of chivalry is not yet gone out of England, and to a man of honour, and a cavalier to boot, but more especially to a British soldier we know, we could not appeal in vain, when we respectfully suggest that an *amende honourable* is unquestionably due to the Rev. Maxwell, of Freetown, Sierra Leone, whom we identify as the black chaplain above referred to: FOR THE OLD MAN'S LIVING YET."

29. S.R.B. Attoh-Ahuma. Ibid. p. 241.

30. Carl Reindorf. *History of Gold Coast and Ashanti*. p 232. Quoted here from S.R.B. Attoh-Ahuma. Ibid. p. 241.

31. R.B. Attoh-Ahuma. Ibid. p. 241.

32. F.L. Bartels. *Jacobus Eliza Capitein 1717-1747. In the Transactions of the Historical Society of Ghana*. Vol. IV. Part 1. Legon. 1959.

33. I.S. Ephson. *Gallery of Gold Coast Celebrities*. Accra. 1969. The above study lacks precision, and apart from its clearly picturesque descriptions, is intellectually shoddy.

Chapter III

Life History

Capitein was born on the 22nd of June, 1717, somewhere in Fantiland; in the present Central Region of Ghana. At the tender age of 8, he was sold to the Dutch sea captain, Arenout Steenhart, who had come to West Africa with the "good ship" *Nieuwenhoven*, anchored in the St. Andreas river in order to purchase slaves and sell other commodities.

Steenhart was presumably an "old coaster" for records suggest that he visited the Gold Coast several times during the 1720s. Indeed in 1723, Steenhart undertook a survey on behalf of the West India Company (Section Zeeland) of the land around Bassam, about 25 miles above Axim in the present day Ghana-Ivory Coast border area. His mission apparently was to assess the possibilities of the area, as a new area for intensive Dutch trade in gold, ivory and slaves. In his report Steenhart revealed that the natives requested the captain to be so kind as to intervene with the honourable (officials of the company) and to ask them to build a fort with 18 cannons to protect the company's trade. If the Dutch would not take up the offer then the natives would be obliged to accept the eager advances of the English.[1] Several of the studies on Capitein appearing in the *Navorscher* in the 19th century suggest that his original name was Asar.[2]

Steenhart presented the youngster, Capitein, as a gift to a pastor in the Dutch controlled post at Shama, Jacobus van Goch. It was van Goch who gave the African boy the name Capitein. Eekhof suggests that this was presumably because he, van Goch, had received the boy from a ship captain.[3] On the 14th of April 1728, van Goch and Capitein travelled with Steenhart on the latter's ship, *Brandenburg*, and on the 25th of

July, 1728, entered Middleburg in Zeeland, from where they, van Goch and Capitein, moved further north on to van Goch's hometown, The Hague. Later Capitein penned praise verses about The Hague and Holland, and went so far as comparing the *Haagsche Bos* to the jungles of Africa. In The Hague, Capitein was virtually entrusted to pastor Johan Philip Manger for his early religious education. Manger and his wife, Sara Elizabeth Meinertzhagen, who were both well respected for their cosmopolitan attitudes, provided diligently protective material and emotional support to the young Capitein. Certainly, Capitein must have needed this; for, naturally as a socially spotlighted, visually outstanding lonely African boy in Europe, during an age of relative ignorance and prejudice, his experience or rather, ordeal, must have been emotionally, extraordinarily taxing. For this was an age during which with respect to Africans, the most outlandish cock-and-bull stories circulated in Europe. It was on the basis of these strange stories about Guinea, that most people were opinionated. In Holland of the time, Capitein must have experienced reaction based on these false presumptions. Those who knew the coast, were often more careful in their pronouncements about Africa and Africans. In the preface to his famous book, *Nauwkeri Beschrijving van de Guinese goud, tand, en slaven-kust* (1704): translated into English as *A New and Accurate Description of the Coast of Guinea* (1704), Willem Bosman draws the reader's attention to these realities. He wrote:

> But 'twas an ancient saying among the Romans, that Africa always produces something New; and to this Day the saying is very just; for the Coast of Guinea, which is part of Africa is for the most part unknown, not only to the Dutch, but to all Europeans, and no particular Description of it is yet to come to light; nor indeed anything but a few scraps scattered in Books written upon other Subjects, most of which are contrary to Truth, and afford but a sorry Sketch of Guinea.

In appreciation of Manger's support, Capitein wrote a Latin eulogy of 80 lines in praise of Manger when the latter died in 1741.[4]

Capitein followed his catechism under Manger with two sons of a gentleman by the name of Willem Hendrik van Schuylenburch. It was one of these two young Schuylenburch's who informed yet another young man, one of the sons of the pastor, Hendrik Velse, that Capitein was,

> interested in studying theology, and then going back to Africa and with God's help, drawing his countrymen from their idolatry and introducing them to the true religion.[5]

All this got to the ear of Hendrik Velse. Velse had particular interest in missionary work among non-Christian people. In 1739 he published a study of Christian missionary work along the coast of Coromandel and Malabar. He therefore, gave very sympathetic ear and response to Capitein's aspirations, and undertook contact with van Goch in order to secure approval for Capitein's formal education. Having obtained this, Velse took Capitein into his house and also sent him to the Latin School. Obviously his exceptional circumstance must have invited helpful and useful attention from people who were kindly disposed because we are informed that his headmaster, Isaac Valkenaar, was singularly attentive to the educational needs of his black pupil. Another mentor was a Dutch woman of aristocratic birth, Jonkvrouw F.C. Roscam. Anna Maria Schuurman taught Capitein Latin, Greek, and Hebrew. Through Roscam, Capitein met the jurist Pieter Cunaeus, one of the people who later recommended him to Leyden University. Capitein was baptised on the 8th July, 1735. It was on this ceremonious occasion that he received the names Jacobus, Eliza, Johannes. We are told that the first name Jacobus, was given in honour of his benefactor van Goch, Eliza in honour of van Goch's sister, and Johannes a niece of van Goch. Obviously the newsworthiness of a blackamoor being baptised in Holland at that time must have been considerable. One Marten Smets in reaction to this spectacular happening, wrote excited verse, part of which, freely translated reads as follows:

> Who has ever heard a thing like this, in days gone by, A moor baptised with Philip's baptismal water. Now that Philip Manger has given the baptismal certificate to Capitein, a moor, for ever shall he live in the clear light of truth.

Capitein ended his six and a half year school run, with an open lecture on the theme: *De Vocatione Ethnicorum* (The Calling of the Gentiles). Here, he displayed insight and dedication to Christian missionary work. He proved in the open his ability theoretically to perform as a missionary and apparently won the support and approval of his mentors. It is important to bear in mind the fact that these people within Dutch society who operated as Capitein's benefactors, were not isolated individuals. They were most probably, connected in the sense that they probably were elements related directly or indirectly, to the Dutch West India Company. In the Netherlands of the time, the social and economic influence of the Dutch West India Company, was to say the least, considerable. And it is not improbable that many of his views about the then nature of things, particularly in terms of the relations between Africa and Europe, were shaped by views in vogue among those social and economic elements operating within the ideological orbit of the Dutch West India Company.

The *Album Studiosorum Academiae Lugduno-Batavae* informs us that on the 12th June 1737, at the youthful age of 20, Capitein entered Leyden University as a student of theology, registered by the Rector Magnificus, Johannes Jacobus Vitrarius. Then, even more than now, Leyden University was a haven for both scholarship and Dutch aristocrats. University life for the *Herren Studenten* was a glorious period of graceful and self-assured hedonistic existence, and for many, the cultivation of bacchanalian tendencies, patrician mores, and a sense of effortless superiority, went hand-in-hand with the rigorous scholarly pursuits on the Rapenburg. Capitein surely, had a good dose of the latter, although there is little evidence as to whether he had any of the sweet and evil life.

The economics of his study was taken care of through a number of sources. In his will, van Goch, who had died in 1734, left Capitein his silver pocket watch, a highly coveted commodity of Leyden students. Further, van Goch instructed his two trustees and inheritors, namely his sister, Elizabeth and Catharina, to see to it that Capitein is well taken care of with respect to his food, drinks, clothing and other necessary equipment. Also they were instructed to provide and see to it that Capitein enjoyed an education in the classics, Latin, Greek and Hebrew plus theology, and that ultimately, Capitein should return to West Africa "to further seek his fortune". Other supporters of Capitein were the *Curatores Haganae Scholar*, the *Edele Mogende Heeren Raaden — Hof van Holland, Regeerders van de stad's-Gravenhage*, Professor Johan van den Honert, and Petrus Cunaeus, who as one of the *Maecenaten* of the Hallet Foundation — Leiden, approved an annual study award of 150 guilders per year for Capitein, on the condition that the latter, on completing his studies should return to West Africa, to preach the gospel. Capitein, on his request, in 1741 got a one year extension of his bursary. He earmarked part of this money for the acquisition of necessities for West Africa. No doubt Capitein had some of the most economically and socially resourceful elements in Dutch society behind him. Silvanus[6] makes a noteworthy observation in this respect when he says that these benefactors were certainly of influence on Capitein's choice of topic for a dissertation.

> We cannot doubt this. Capitein had as a truly lucky kid experienced all imaginable and unexpected results of his slave state. Out of this arose in him a feeling of thankfulness towards his benefactors, the owners of the West India Company. However noble these shareholders were, as typical Dutch merchants of the period, the last thing they would have wished was the

abolition of slavery in the lands overseas. And now Capitein became their defender. Their consciences could thus be set to rest.

Further evidence of the pressure of forces in the West India Company on the choice of thesis and argument presented therein can be obtained from the preface to his thesis. The evidence could not be more telling. He wrote that,

> Very often, I have noted that some Christians are worried that because of the message of freedom of the Christian Gospel, plantation slavery which was instituted by Christians may be abolished to the great financial loss of the Directors of the West India Company. There have been people, yes, there are still people in the Christian world, especially in the Netherlands, who activated by a spirit unknown to me, argue that Christian freedom is contrary to slavery. My present state of affairs demands that I prove, that this idea has grown either out of ignorance of the true spirit of the gospel, or out of superstition.

On the 10th of March, 1742, Capitein defended his thesis *Dissertatio Politico-Theologica de Servitute libertati Christiane non contraria* in Latin in the Pieterskerk, Leiden.[7] With this academic exercise completed, Capitein was quickly put through the processes of ordainment as a pastor of the Reformed Church in Amsterdam. After doing a number of examinations he was finally pronounced minister of the gospel in May 1742, by the Church Council, Classis of Amsterdam. Capitein was made to promise correspondence with the Church authorities in Amsterdam about his progress and activities in Elmina. Capitein's first sermon as a full pastor, took place in the Pieterskerk, Leiden, and then after that, in Middleburg and Muiderberg. He then spent some time in Ouderkerk-aan-den-Amstel in the villa of a certain Willem Backer, one of the prominents among the

Directors of the West India Company. Here, Capitein met his employers whom he thanked. These *Bewindhebberen van de West-Indische Compagnie* must have also taken the opportunity to size up their employee. Thus, after 14 years stay in Holland, Capitein was sufficiently and elaborately, ideologically groomed to go back to West Africa to preach the holy script, but this, fundamentally, in the service of the same economic and social forces which had brought him originally to the Netherlands. These forces were, in fact, the interests of the *West Indische Compagnie*, then an outstandingly essential pillar in developing Dutch capitalism. Capitein was showered with praise and farewells, some cast in contemporary poetical forms. One admirer wrote:

> God was your protector
> O wonder of wonders
> O Capitein, trained
> By the great Honert
>
> When God called early
> Through storms and dangers
> Brought through the briny ocean
> On Eagle's wings
>
> In Leiden's famous school
> You whiled away your time
> On linguistic expressions
> Nothing was beyond you
>
> Long may your valiant mind
> In full splendour bloom
> Your knowledge of God grow
> O glory of Africa.[8]

One of Capitein's friends, a medical student from Leiden University claimed to have had a vision, in which *Pallas Athene* appeared to him in a somber and mournful mood. The poet asked *Pallas Athene* the reason for such great sadness, to which the vision replied:

43

You ask what has made me so sad
It is that, a young man in whom I have
always had pleasure, and loved so much
Is leaving me soon; O disaster
Capitein my dear friend,
Who I can describe as a pearl in my crown
Yes, who the University always will boast of
To have had within its walls
Will you, O dearest! leave my city?[28]

Yet another admirer of Capitein wrote:

Farewell, O wonder of our times!
To still have a courageous Capitein
With belief in Jesus;
Will keep the Netherlands pleased.[8]

He left the Netherlands on the 18th of July 1742. At the
age of 25, Capitein was back in West Africa. He touched the
sunny coast on the 8th October, 1742. He arrived in the
slave ship *De Catharina Galey*. The ship captain was Andries
Graan. The ship *De Catharina Galey* was under instructions
from the West India Company to collect a cargo of about
550 slaves from Elmina, and transport them to the West
Indies. Indeed reports of the company indicate that the cargo
of slaves were duly "loaded" but only about 330 of the
approximately 550 slaves were safely landed alive in
Curacao.[9] In Elmina, Capitein was, of course, being
inquisitively awaited. The Commander of the post at Elmina
was Jacob de Petersen. Exactly a fortnight after Capitein's
arrival (22nd October, 1742), Jacob de Petersen wrote
enthusiastically about the new arrival and his work to the
directors of the company. Capitein had also, the previous
day, in a letter to his employers in Holland, commented on
the "friendliness and affection" with which he has been
received by Director-General Jacob de Petersen. In his, as it
were, official inaugural sermon, which took place also on the
21st October, 1742, in the church of·the castle, Capitein
spelt out that his tasks were on the one hand, to strengthen

the Christian resolve for eternal life of the Dutch personnel and, on the other, to help his fellow Africans to emerge from their heathen darkness and follow the Christian gospel.

During this period, along the stretch of the Gold Coast, the Dutch West India Company had 241 people in its service of which 107 were in Elmina. Capitein was one of the few and rare Africans in any senior position of employment. Records of the period suggest there was one other local, a mulatto, Thomas Willemse, who was drummer in the adjacent Fort Coenraadsburg.[10] As Eekhof indicates, it is interesting to note that this European colony in West Africa was not predominantly Dutch. Although run for and by the West-Indische Compagnie, this collection of Europeans included people from Danzig, Oldenburg, Hesse, Leipzig, Ghent, Brussels, Mecklenburg, Cologne and other places. This variety of European nationals belonged to widely different Christian Churches, and this made Capitein's work in the end difficult. Faced with the problem of growing absence from catechism by many of the Europeans at the Elmina post, Capitein later wrote that,

> most of those here are Roman Catholics or Lutherans, and the Reformed are always too occupied with their daily business.[11]

Boxer informs us that:

> The role of Calvinism in the African possessions of the West India Company can like-wise ... be dismissed in a few lines[12]

Capitein's immediate predecessor pastor at Elmina had been Isaacus Ketelanus who had been given the sack by the West-Indische Compagnie on the 29th of October 1734, on account of his misconduct and bad behaviour.

As pastor in charge of the Elmina post, Capitein was a full employee of the West-Indische Compagnie. He received a payment of 100 guilders per month, plus rations. Apart from his regular pastoral work, Capitein within a month of his arrival started a school for the pure African and mulatto (*tapoejers*), and a couple of European kids. He was helped in this successively by the teachers (lay-readers), Abraham Suurdeeg, Jan Boying, Pieter Ernestus Schutsler and Adrian van Waghem. The school had a daily average of between 18 and 20 pupils, mainly boys. We are told by Eekhof that most of them could, in 5 months, go through their A.B.C. alphabet, the 12 Articles of Belief, the Lord's Prayer and the 10 Commandments. The West-Indische Compagnie provided equipment and books. All in all, his first year was satisfactory. In 1743 his problems from all directions started mounting. Getting children to come to his school was becoming steadily difficult. He made a special effort to convince the elders of Elmina to send their children to school to be christianized. He explained that this was the policy of the West India Company, they were obliged to comply to this aim of the company "without further delay, being subjects" of the company. After this the number of school children increased to 45.

The then Ashantihene Opoku Ware, having been impressed by Capitein's own education in Holland decided to send 12 boys and 2 girls to the Netherlands through the West-Indische Compagnie. Opoku Ware forwarded this request to de Petersen, and added 10 elephant tusks as payment. De Petersen decided, however, that the job should be done on the spot in Elmina under Capitein's auspices. Opoku Ware insisted that the 10 elephant tusks be sent by ship with an African supervisor of these gifts to be given to the *Bewindhebberen* (Directors) of the West Indische Compagnie. In return Opoku Ware requested a glass-sided coffin. De Petersen personally placed an order with his agents, *Lohoff and Gebrs. Ploots* of Amstel near Amsterdam for the coffin, and a youngster, Gyekye, was sent as escort with the elephant tusks on board the slaveship *Maria Galey* to the Netherlands.

About a year after Capitein's arrival at Elmina, he fell in love with an African girl from Elmina. In a letter written on the 15th of February, 1743, by Capitein to the *Bewindhebberen der West-Indische Compagnie*, after an introductory paragraph of polite language, Capitein went on to inform his employers that:

> For the happy continuation now and the quick achievement of my great aim, I have after lengthy consultation about issues, reached the conclusion that, it would not be unsound if I legally married a young black girl, who was not only born here in Elmina, but proven to be more suitable and competent than most for education. In this way, I would win the trust and confidence of the black people here in Elmina, because they would then see that although I differ from them in lifestyle and religion, I am not alienated from them, that rather, my presence here is in their interest.

He added also, that this marriage would help him further to resist better "the temptations of Satan". Capitein went on to point out that having found the girl, he informed the Director-General de Petersen and the girl's parents. He, Capitein, had also inquired from de Petersen if it was possible to first marry the young woman and then educate and convert her to Christianity. On this issue de Petersen consulted the Edict of the West-India Company. This revealed that it was not possible to first marry her and then educate her. The procedure was that the girl should first be educated and baptised, the question remained as to who was to be her educator? Capitein pointed out that neither the Church Reader Adrianus van Waghem nor he Capitein, of course, could undertake the girl's education, and there was unfortunately no Dutch woman available as an educator for Capitein's projected wife. Capitein informs us in his letter, that the Director-General of the Elmina post, de Petersen, suggested that the girl be sent to the Netherlands for her education. This suggestion was in turn unacceptable to the parents of the girl, who felt that Capitein should marry their daughter and then educate and convert her.

It is interesting and important to note that in that particular letter, Capitein threw up his undigested love life.

It closes with an ironical sentence which underwrote economic and ideological dependence on the West India company. His words are that;

> while matters rest so, I consider it my duty, to wait for you (Director of the West India Company) for further orders.

Presumably as a pastor in the pay of the West India Company, he had to adopt this line of action, and, indeed, await the views and opinions of his masters. These contradictions emphasize the fact that his whole relationship with his own people had to be regulated from outside, by people and forces whose economic and social progress was based on an impersonal, historically created system, which often separated mother and child, father and son, brother and sister, through slavery, in order to make record profits.

Capitein was still unrebellious, and prepared to bend to the utmost to meet the requirements of those who held him in fee. His evangelical work was less fruitful than he cared to admit. How long was this to last? While not decisively making a break with his employers, Capitein apparently continued to push forward his own piecemeal solutions, because two months later, in a letter dated 18th April, 1743, forwarded to *de Bewindhebberen der West-Indische Compagnie*, Capitein wrote that,

> concerning the young black woman of whom I spoke in my last letter, and about whom I expressed my wish for further orders, on whether it would be in order for me to first marry her and then educate her, (now without the preliminary education) since she, together with other full-blooded black and mulatto pupils of her age, are attending the school, and can be lawfully prepared for my objective.

The Classis in Amsterdam was displeased with Capitein's plans and moves. The classis further strongly resented the fact that Capitein had not kept to the arrangement of regular correspondence with the classis. In a letter dated 10th January, 1745, the classis expressed its dissatisfaction with Capitein's "bad behaviour". In a meeting which took place on the 12th of January, 1745, the classis decided to adopt certain sanctions (*deputati ad res exteras*).

In reply to the letter of the classis, Capitein, on the 21st of May 1746, pointed out to the classis that he had not corresponded because, in the first place, his instructions indicated that depending on the conditions and specifics of the situation and its effect on the religion, reports should be made to the *Bewindhebberen*. Secondly, there was no organised parish as such. Thirdly, he understood that the West-Indische Compagnie and the classis were in contact. After all, his initial report on his church and school work had not been replied to. This report apparently had provoked the anger of many people mainly, employees of the West Indische Compagnie on the Gold Coast. Capitein went on to inform the classis that, regarding his love affair and plans to marry the Elmina girl, "God who sees all", has indeed provided a solution. A Dutch Girl had been brought on a company ship. This girl was chaperoned by the family of Jan Credo Bacot. She was, as they say, a "Haagse", a woman from the Hague, and called Antonia Genderdros. The first marriage proclamation was made on the 3rd October. The second and third proclamations and the marriage took place on the 10th October, 1745; and the Director-General of the castle de Petersen, gave a special party in honour of the couple.

In a treaty that was signed between the Elminas, the other Fantis in the area, and the West India Company on the 3rd of September 1744, Capitein featured as an interpreter for the parties concerned. Capitein translated the Lord's Prayer, the 10 Commandments, and the Creed or 12 Articles of Belief into Fanti. This 20-page book, published in 1744, contained also a preface written by Capitein for the Christian reader.

It is interesting to note that Capitein, in his translation of the 10 Commandments, when he came to the 4th

Commandment, according to the Classis in Amsterdam, failed to mention that also servants and slaves should rest on the Sabbath. Was this also an attempt on his part to defend the interests of the W.I.C. against the lot of slaves? Because of this omission, the Classis recommended that the whole page be reprinted. The Classis also pointed out that he had wrongly translated "Our Father" as "Father of us all".

Capitein actually discovered through records that, indeed the religious life official and unofficial, of the Elmina post was deplorable. The church records in Elmina dated from 1683; however, huge gaps existed in them. This discovery must have been, of course, very uninspiring for Capitein. The castle community of European colonists was not the sort of group to take religion seriously. They tended to be rough and ready types who took advantage of their absence from their countries of origin, where social control and sanctions for them were more effective. Such far-flung outposts as Elmina tended to collect a motley of bizarre elements, "the dregs of Dutch society" and "louts from the depths of Germany". It was fairly common for elements like these, to run into conflict with ecclesiastics. The ecclesiastics, on the other hand, on the whole did not have the best of reputations. They tended to be regarded as arrogant and overbearing, characteristics which are not in keeping with the fundamental attitudinal requirements of their holy office.[13] As a black man, Capitein suffered the extra scorn, jealousy, and contempt of the European colonists. Even today, in this era of relative enlightenment, blacks continue to be insulted and oppressed all over the world wherever they live with whites.

In the 18th century, with slavery and all, European racial arrogance was rabid. This ideological superstructure rested on an economic substructure of West European mercantile capitalism of which the Atlantic slave trade in Africans was a principal feature. Capitein was a victim of European racism. Eekhof writes that:

> It cannot be denied that the employees
> (bureaucrats in the service of the company)

frequently treated him roughly. In any case, how could these white colonists respect such as African Moor, in spite of his having studied in Europe! Among them was, principally, the treasurer Huibert van Rijk, who both in public and in the presence of members of the church council, spoke denigratingly about the predikant and religion, saying that he came to church only out of curiosity.[14]

In sum, a number of factors conspired against the efficient and sustained development of Capitein's work in Elmina. After a time, these factors tended to erode his resolve and break his will to continue. Principal among these factors was the uncooperativeness of the European colonists in Elmina. They snubbed and humiliated him on the basis of his racial origin while he was supposed to live and work among them. Secondly, in these far-away outposts, as pointed out earlier, these colonists shunned religious life, and the ecclesiastics themselves were not always the best in chaste and exemplar existence. In his letter to the Presidential Chamber Zeeland of the West India Company, dated 1st April, 1747, apart from informing the directors of the company that Capitein had passed away on the 1st of February, the Governor de Petersen indicated that although it is true that some of the employees behaved badly towards Capitein, the roots of Capitein's problems was his predilection for commerce. De Petersen points out that Capitein was advised to stay away from these practices but to no avail. His commercial activities apparently eroded his christian missionary zeal, and left him little diligence to pursue his evangelical work. Some idea of the extent of his debts can be obtained from the *Navorscher* of 1877. On the 13th of May 1746, Capitein made out a bond to Nikolaas Matthias van der Noot de Gietere for 2528 Florins and 15 Stuivers, to be drawn from his salary paid by the West India Company. On the 27th of December 1746, Capitein was summoned by court order and ordered to pay the sum owed to Nikolaas Matthias van der Noot De Gietere. Again on the same day another debt of F.1850.00 owed to Jurian in Amsterdam was enforced by a power of attorney granted to the ship captain Lindenberg. Still another outstanding debt was brought to light on the same day which indicated that for a debt owed to Simon van Buuren of F.5225 dated 1st October 1741, only F.2400.00 had so far been paid. Simon van Buuren, a surgeon in the employ of the West India Company had come to Elmina, to pursue legal proceedings against Capitein. Van Buuren remarked that he had little trust in the pastor. Capitein is reported to have said: "I do not have it; sell my bed, it's no shame to me. Let those who wish to claim money be anxious, and not those in debt". Apparently Capitein claimed that his wife was in agreement with him. Capitein is reported further to have said that:

> What does Van Buuren mean, that I should limit what appears on my dining table and keep my tummy on short rations in order to satisfy him. No, I would not do that, I would not do that![15]

These are not the only debts of Capitein which come to light. In a legal act issued on the 30th December 1746, we are informed that apart from the above mentioned debts, he owed Alexander Jacob, an Elmina innkeeper F.1200.00, Hendrik van Keulen, a wine trader in Amsterdam, F.79.00. Thus by the end of 1746, Capitein was up to his neck in debt which he undertook to pay "as time goes on" out of his salary.

His problems with the Classis and the authorities of the W.I.C. must have been also quite disheartening to say the least, and the total impact of his constant difficulties must have created some measure of crisis of confidence among the African population. Surprisingly in the face of all his difficulties, in his letters to the *Bewindhebberen* he continued to give the impression that he was diligently pursuing his original duties. On the 1st July, 1745, he wrote to the *Bewindhebberen* a request to resign from his duties. Instead, he was sent provisions, ham, tobacco, pipes, red and white wines and various types of liquors. Capitein died on the 1st of February 1747, at the age of 30.

Notes

CHAPTER III

1. *Berigt of Relaes Van den Schipper Arenout Steenhart Aan deEdelagtbaar heeren Bewinthebberen Van de geoctroyeerde Westindische Comp: ter Kamer Zeeland. Wegens het Land Bason.* Middleburg. 17 June 1723. Verzamelinge Verspreide West-Indische Stukken. Rijks Archieven. The Hague.

2. The precise origins of the attribution of the name *Asar* to Capitein is not very clear. It could well and truly be his original name, but it could also well be a fabrication or rumour and story-telling. As the name stands it could be understood as a typical Akan name, a misrepresentation of *Ansa*, for such mistaken rendering of African names by Europeans, especially in that period is not uncommon. L. Proes in his note which appeared in the *Navorscher* (1877) informs us that his brother-in-law Governor Nagtglas wrote in the 1860s that: "Asar is completely unknown to me, I have not come across the name anywhere. There is, however, a rumour that an African pastor had later completely turned fetish. But there is no name attributed to the latter". Proes then goes on to argue that: "Now the question is whether Asar can be presumed to be the same person as Capitein. I am inclined to believe that, because it would be an extraordinary coincidence, that two negroes were brought here, wrote the same thesis, and were both sent back to Africa, and again both were lost to civilization. This leads me to conclude that Capitein as a child in Guinea was called Asar".

3. Eekhof. Op cit. p. 145.

4. This was published with Elandus van Staveren's *Lijkreden*. The whole poem is reproduced in English in S.R.B. Attoh-Ahuma's *Memoirs of West African Celebrities*. Liverpool. 1905.

5. Originally from his *Dissertatio Politico-Theologica de Servitute, libertati Christianae non contraria*. p. XIV. But quoted here from Eekhof. Op cit. page 11.

6. Silvanus in A.W. Bronsveld. *Stemmen voor Waarheid en Vrede*. Utrecht. 1891.

7. Eekhof indicates that this was in fact not for a doctorate degree as many commentators on Capitein would have it. See Eekhof pp. 18-19.

8. Freely translated from poem as appears by Silvanus in A. Bronsveld. *Stemmen voor Waarheid en Vrede*. Utrecht. 1891. p. 1096.

9. Reports of the W.I.C. *Verspreide W.I. Stukken*. Rijks Archiven. Den Haag.

10. See *Verspreide West-Indische Stukken* (Rijks Archiven). Den Haag. Payroll list for 1741, written by Jacob de Petersen (October 1741). These records show also that the death rate among Europeans on the coast was very high.

11. Quoted here from C.R. Boxer. *The Dutch Seaborne Empire*. London. 1966. p. 152.

12. C.R. Boxer. Ibid. p. 152.

13. C.R. Boxer. Ibid. p. 5.

14. Eekhof. Op cit. p. 65.

15. *Navorscher*. 1877, pages 50 and 51, quoted from de Petersen, as reported

by Nagtglas. Capitein was probably aware of the fact that various cock-and-bull stories were flying about in the Netherlands about him. The evidence is not conclusive although suggestive. In a reply to a letter from his old university mate Johannes Van Dijk dated 1st July, 1745, (in reply to Van Dijk's letter of 11th February, 1743) Capitein writes that, "Your pleasure about my safe arrival here on this coast and about the happy beginnings of my special purpose and holy office is the gladness of a friend, which makes me see that you are really interested in my welfare. Concerning the lies circulated by Scherping to which you briefly refer; the beginning, progress, and end have been described to me in detail by our learned ..... Schuurmans. I will state no more than that, I have seen and heard ......the mouths of the liars being effectively plugged up, and the judge of this whole earth with whom we have to deal, shall make them perish". (To be found in the Royal Library. The Hague).

Chapter IV

Writings and Speeches

One would have preferred to have more of Capitein's work available today. Although admittedly he was not a voluminous writer, and therefore by way of literary legacy, what exists today is not much; it is sufficiently substantial, to give some impression of the man and his mind. Particularly, if we bear in mind the fact that Capitein died at the youthful age of 30.

His letters, in particular, all of them written after 1742, give a picture of his life in Elmina. In many ways, that was the most dramatic period of his life, and Eekhof's study indicates the present whereabouts of these letters.[1] Stylistically, apart from the rather staid and formalistic mould of the period, Capitein in his choice and arrangement of language tends often to be rather pompous and ponderous, favouring often circuitous and involved turns of language. Today, two centuries later, the language of Capitein's letters rings very quaint, and for the modern reader, reading them provides among other things, exotic pleasures from a bygone age.

Capitein's Akan versions of the Lord's Prayer, the 12 Articles of Belief, and the 10 Commandments were published under the title: *Vertaling van Onze Vader, de Twaalf Geloofs-Artykelen, en de Tien Geboden des Heeren, Uit de Nederduitshe Taal, in de Negersche Spraak, zo als die gebruikelijk is van Abrowarie tot Apam. Doorgaans Letterlijke overgebragt door Jacobus Elisa Joannes Capitein.*[2]

A couple of Capitein's sermons delivered in 1742, shortly

before he left Holland for the Gold Coast and published as *Uitgewrogte Predikatien*,[3] in the same year, have survived him. Both these sermons testify to Capitein's thorough training and his firm grasp of his role as a pastor. These were, *Trouwhertige vermaaninge van de Apostel der Heydenen Paul, aan zijnen zoon Timotheus*, from Timothy 2, verse 8, preached at Muiderberg on the 20th of May 1742; *Alsmeede de voornaamste Goederen van de Opperste Wijsheit* from Proverbs 8, verse 18. Two sermons, preached in The Hague on the 27th of May 1742 and Ouderkerk aan den Amstel on the 6th of June 1742. His inaugural sermon at Elmina, *Het Groote Genadeligt Gods in zijn Dienaaren onder de bediening der Genade*, from 2nd Corinthians 4, verse 6. This was published by Hieronymus de Wilhem in Amsterdam, 1744.

His Latin oration of 1737 *De Vocatione Ethnicorum* was divided into three main parts. Basing himself on biblical writing he developed an argument to back his view of the divine authenticity of the Christian faith and promise, which he saw as embracing all nations and all peoples. However, the unfolding and development of this process, he suggested, is historically slow. He argued further that in order to play a useful and contributory role in the divine scheme and order, the languages of non-christian nations should be developed and learnt. He also advocated the systematic pursuit of missionary activity among these heathen peoples, winning them for Christianity through gentle and patient persuasion. He indicated that the Portuguese and Spaniards have generally been soft and humane in their treatment of slaves, maintaining no entrenched myth of racial superiority. Other slaving nations have denied Christianity to blacks in contradiction to the basic idea of Christian brotherhood and the equality of men. In general tenor, this speech given in 1737, was obviously more liberal in outlook than his thesis of 1742. Between these two dates, his views obviously took a more conservative turn, probably under the influence of conservative teachers and mentors. Capitein also exhibited a modest poetic talent in print. These poems do not display exceptional artistic qualities as such, but are technically well-written in the accepted styles of the period. Perhaps particularly significant from Capitein's poetic work, were firstly, his 80 line elegy to Philip Manger (1741) which was first published in Elandus van Staveren's *Lijkreden* and subsequently appeared with his thesis. Secondly, his two poems written (1742), one of which was dedicated and written for his friend Brandijn Ryser.[4]

Capitein's thesis is a slim scholarly piece, very well and firmly rooted in the classics. An intelligent mind, it is tragically ironical that his intellectual equipment was subtly used to justify slavery when he himself had been a slave child. Presumably it attracted considerable and fairly extended interest, for apart from the original Latin text, at least four editions of the work were published in Dutch. Apart from its obviously "attractive" title, as his biographer Silvanus has pointed out:

> The thesis displays scholarship. In the typical schoolish genre of his time, full of rhetoric, as if it was a spiritual tournament, and furthermore abundantly furnished with humorous quotations from both ecclesiastical and profane writers. This work gives no small impression of the richness of his scholarship, and the wit of this African moor. Albeit he remains the devil's advocate.[5]

The author began by laying down a definitional premise to slavery as a social institution. He argued that slavery;

> is not a voluntary contract, by which two or more people bind themselves mutually in such a way that one party serves the other, to be remunerated with food and other subsistence requirements, and the other party imposes work. It is more correct to describe someone who serves this way as a servant or hand, and not a slave; what the Greeks call a *misthoton*. We understand by slavery in agreement with the definition of jurists, someone who, against his will, is placed under the authority of someone else. This person should strictly speaking be called a slave or serf. We see the point

perfectly distinguished in my opinion by Seneca ...

Continuing, Capitein, asserted that the core of the problem to which he addresses himself in the thesis is,

> whether with respect to evangelical freedom, it is justifiable for Christians to possess other people as their own property; in such a way that, although those people (the slaves) may subscribe to the teaching of the Christian religion, in actual fact, in so far as the body is concerned, they are and remain subjugated in slavery.

In order to argue his case systematically, Capitein divided his exposé in two main parts. In the first part, he set out to investigate the origins of slavery as a historically formed institution, and attempted to show that slavery is a universal institution; prevalent at one stage or the other, among all people. In the second part, Capitein set out to prove that slavery is not contrary to Christianity.

In the opening of the second chapter of his study, Capitein proposed that every mortal, according to natural law is his own boss, that is to say that, the normal condition of original man, the first humans, was freedom and equality. This to him, is not doubted by any authority. The reason being that we are in origin all equal. Capitein elaborated on this point and then proceeded to point out that in the light of his views, he dismisses the polemics of Aristotle in the first book of Politics, 5th chapter, that in the natural state itself, distinction between people is recognized so that one is born free and the other a slave. Capitein added that these ideas of Aristotle had been rejected even by other pagans, although in their investigations of the origins of slavery, they are divided in different ways and they had come close "to the guiding torch of truth". They believed slavery to have originated from their unjust repression, or coincidence, or "in the laws of peoples". Slavery did not exist through the laws of nature, but through human conditions and historical coincidence.

Capitein made an examination of the classical work of Aristotle, Seneca, Horace, Bizetus, Amenopoulos, and contended that slavery followed soon after the floods of Noah's time, as Moses has summarized (Genesis 9, verse 25). Here, it is pointed out that, the argument has been that this miserable state, slavery, was imposed on the descendants of Ham, so that they will always bear the sign of punishment because they had derided the nudity of his father. So that he will be the serf of the serf of his brothers. Capitein argued that slavery is common to most societies, being maintained by such institutions as war-captivity, domestic slavery, and the commercialization of men, he then went on to examine the origins of slavery among the ancient Israelites, Canaanites, and Romans. He quoted further biblical sources on the juridical status of the slave among the Hebrews and indicated that among the latter, a mistreated slave could claim his freedom.

It was in the 3rd chapter that Capitein built his argument that the institution of human bondage is not against Christianity. In the first paragraph of this chapter, he opened up his attack that:

> It is too well-known to be doubted that very many people in the Netherlands want to convince themselves and others in their discussions, that evangelical freedom can in no way coexist with slavery proper. The argument is that in our era, faith must necessarily be not only within a pure soul (the spiritual principle from which it lives, does not submit to the dominance of the devil) but also within a free body.

Capitein dismissed these ideas and their sources, and made a distinction between (a) Spiritual, and (b) Bodily freedom. He points out that in the Netherlands indeed, slavery does not exist; that any slave who comes to Holland automatically becomes free if he embraces Christianity. Capitein argued that the New Testament does not present a case in favour of both physical and spiritual freedom.

59

Throughout the third chapter of his thesis, the author refuted opposing arguments and positions of other authorities, and in the 11th paragraph of this chapter, he hammered home some of his key points. He wrote that:

> So we distinguish between slavery of conscience and sin, from civil slavery; the law of heaven and that of the earthly court of law; and finally a spiritual freedom from bodily freedom: So that Christ speaks of heavenly law and spiritual slavery of conscience from which we are redeemed under the New Testament.

Further, Capitein illustrated his arguments with the biblical case of the slave who fled from his master, became converted, and subsequently returned to his master, again as a slave (letter of Paul to Philemon). This case was for Capitein, obviously indicative of someone who had understood well the difference between spiritual and bodily freedom. Capitein suggested that the New Testament portrays Christ as the head of the spiritual kingdom, and the believers as the subjects, using this picture Capitein inferred that relations of dominance could not be regarded as forbidden, according to Christianity. He went on to say that, if Christianity was to be opened to slaves, many would lie that they have become Christianized in order to gain their physical freedom. Arguing against those who free slaves, Capitein insisted that it was not a pious deed to liberate slaves. Discussing Constantine the Great's laws on the emancipation of slaves, Capitein considered these regulations and ways of freeing slaves to be recent (312-316 A.D.). He added that Constantine had extra-humanitarian reasons for supporting so actively, the emancipation of slaves. Capitein believed that no obligatory reasons could be found for the freeing of slaves, the act of freeing a slave being totally dependent on the wishes of the master, also the absence of slavery in Holland had purely political and no theological grounding. Indeed, the author argued that the real reasons why slavery came to an end in Holland was to be found in the social ethos of the struggle against Spain during the War of Independence. Capitein towards the end of his thesis argued that:

> it is very certain that with the abolition of the institution of slavery, countless inconveniences would be created.

Capitein's thesis is a short and punchy piece of exercise. It is interesting to see Capitein in the role of the "devil's advocate", he is brisk and mentally agile. He makes altogether a swift defence of his case. Thoroughly idealist in approach, he remains completely untouched by the pre-Marxian materialism of the Enlightenment. For this, he was a generation too young, in any case his calling did not lend itself easily to this. So rather, Capitein was an idealist of the 18th century romantic type. His defence of slavery exteriorises this. For an eloquent and westernized former slave-child defending the infamous institution, there was an implicit ideological admiration for strong passions, and a tendency to exaggerate. It came out in the form of his major prop; that is, the categorisation of spiritual and bodily freedom. The spiritual obviously capable of a separate and autonomous existence from the physical body. The fundamental assumption being that consciousness does not derive from matter.

In that particular piece, in sum, he displays a literal and formalistic tendency to sermonise; pedantism, and fundamentally idealist religious dogmatism prevails in his discussions. This is the intellectual substance of his infamous advocacy of that institution slavery, condemned by mankind and time.

Of course, in this as in all others he was a child of his period; a product of social material forces which formed him. All the same Capitein's views were against the tide of history. A mere 43 years later in 1785, an Englishman Thomas Clarkson won a Latin prize at Cambridge University on the subject: "Is it right to make slaves of others against their will?" He found a different meaning to the Christian inspiration claiming that he had experienced a "direct revelation from God ordering him to devote his life to abolishing the trade" In fact it is not as if Capitein would have been the first to condemn slavery in the Netherlands if he had done so, instead of his pathetic arguement in favour of the inhuman trade. In his own profession as a clergyman, indeed within his own protestant denomination, Godfried Cornelis Udemans the Hervormde pastor of Zierikzee in his *'t Geestelijck Roer van't Coopmans schip* (1640) at least a good hundred years before Capitein, had sought to establish what he considered to be principal conditions for legitimate slavery in Dutch colonies. His idea was that slaves should not be sold to the Portuguese and Spanish since that would expose them to Catholicism. In Dutch colonies, he suggested that slaves should be Christianized, and once they have been drawn to the "true faith", after some years of loyal service, they should be set free. Udemans' view was that no Hervormde should hold another Hervormde in slavery.[6] Before Udemans, the famous Dutch jurist Hugo de Groot argued in his *De jure belli ac pacis* (1625) that slavery was against natural law.

Notes

CHAPTER IV

1. A. Eekhof: *De Negerpredikant*, 1917.
2. A. Eekhof: Ibid. p. 59. Translated into English the title reads: Translation of the Lord's Prayer, the 12 Articles of Belief, and the Ten Commandments, from the Low-German language, into the Negro language, as spoken from Abrowarie to Apam. Put in this written form by Jacobus Elisa Joannes Capitein.
3. This work can be found in the University Library, Leiden.
4. See *Verzameling van Lof, Lijk — en Mengelgedichten* (No. 71 K.C.) in the Provincial Library of Zeeland (Middleburg), Netherlands. The poem to P. Manger appears in English, in S.R.B. Attoh-Ahuma's *Memoirs of West African Celebrities*. Liverpool. 1905.
5. Silvanus. In A.W. Bronsveld. *Stemmen voor Waarheid en Vrede*. Utrecht. 1891. p. 1089.
6. See P.J. Meertens. *Godfriedus Cornelisz Udemans*. Nederlandsch Archief voor Kerkgeschiedenis 28. 1936.pp. 65-106. Also G.F. de Jong. The Dutch Reformed Church and Negro Slavery in Colonial America. *Church History*. Vol. 40. 1971. pp. 423-436.

Chapter V

Rambling Historical Considerations

The bourgeois Dutch state was born towards the end of the 16th century. Of course, as a cultural area the Dutch language has a much longer tradition and source in the "low countries by the sea" (to borrow an expression of Jan Romein).[1] From the 6th century A.D., during the period of the Frankish migrations this cultural area developed, and neither the present late capitalist Dutch state nor the 16th century state created to serve fundamentally a fledgling anti-papist merchant bourgeoisie caught up in the process of early capitalist accumulation actually corresponds to the real cultural linguistic territorial area.[2] During the middle ages, the area of present-day Netherlands was fragmented into variously sized duchies, counties, and bishoprics. The feudal rulers within their fiefdoms ruled supreme. Although after 1384, the House of Burgundy managed to achieve a partially integrated polity out of the previously disparate feudal entities, this new political structure remained largely feudal in fundamental structure and as such the parts of this partially integrated polity maintained their essential individual socio-political organisation.

The Hapsburgs, who acceded the Burgundians controlled an empire which was based, politically in Spain, and extended from North Europe into the southern hemisphere of the Americas. Heavy taxation, the elevation of Spanish nobles to leading positions, the chauvinism of Philip II, the excesses of the inquisition, and fundamentally the slow but steady growth of bourgeois interests in the low countries culminated in the revolt of the Netherlands. The revolt triumphed in the north of the Netherlands but failed in the south. Thus, the Netherlands gained its independence from Spain as a result of the bourgeois revolution of 1566-1609. In substance, the revolt was both a struggle waged by the emergent bourgeoisie and popular classes against feudalist absolutism, and was at the same time a war for national liberation and independence. The war against Spain dragged on into the first decade of the 17th century when, in 1609, after a number of decisive battles, Spain recognized the independence of the bourgeois Dutch state. The state was considerably centralized, and each of the seven constituent provinces sent representatives to the federal parliament, the States-General in the Hague. Provincial autonomy was largely maintained in fiscal and judicial matters, and apart from this, the socio-economic centres of power tended to vary from province to province, in the sense that whereas, the provinces of Zeeland and Holland were dominated by an urban bourgeois class of merchants, in rural Gelderland, Overijssel, or Utrecht, feudal power remained relatively dominant. The dominant class of merchant patricians have been variously called Heeren *(Gentlemen)*, *Regenten* (Regents). Its closed and in-bred character reinforced its oligarchical and caste-like tendencies. Within the state, Holland remained principal, and it has been estimated; that it contributed 58% of the federal budget.[3]

Thus, the key role the province of Holland played in the economic and political life of the state rested on the activities of this mercantile bourgeois class. The mercantilist period, mainly from the late 16th to the late 18th century was such that, the main trading nations of the world, Spain, Holland, France and England, had built up colonial empires of world-wide scope, a process involving frequent armed conflict between two or more of the participants. The underlying purposes of the colonial system were mainly to ensure the safety and property of the merchants engaged in the colonial trade through primarily monopolistic chartered trading companies. Also to exclude the competition of foreign merchants, and shippers; and to regulate the terms of trade between mother country and colony in such a way as to ensure that the lion's share of the benefit w uld accrue to the former. Mercantilism was thus characterised by the pursuit of an active and aggressive colonial policy.

Early in the 17th century, by sheer dint of their then superior development of productive forces, advanced commercial organisation, and technique, the relative economic underdevelopment of their neighbours, and also their particularly favourable geographical position, the Dutch effectively achieved clear supremacy in European commerce and transport and a national prosperity unparalleled in Dutch history; either before or after that time. Till this present day, the Dutch public is considerably fed and nourished with inspirational sentiments and symbols rooted in that era of Dutch global glory. The Dutch *Gouden Eeuw* (Golden Age) is usually considered to have spanned the latter half of the 17th century and the beginning of the 18th century. In 1728, the year Capitein was taken to Holland, Defoe described the Dutch as;

> the carriers of the world, the middle Persons in Trade, the Factors and Brokers of Europe ... they buy to sell again, take in to send out: and the Greatest Part of their Commerce consists in being supply'd from all parts of the world again.[4]

Indeed, for a great part of the 18th century, Amsterdam functioned as the central granary for supplying the Mediterranean with grain originally obtained from the Baltic. In the opposite direction, went wine and fruits, Germany and France supplied textiles and wines. Italy supplied silks, cotton was obtained from the Levant, metal from Austria and Sweden, spice and colonial goods from the seaborne empire.[5] Marx minces no words when he relates that:

The colonial systems ripened, like a hot-house trade............ The colonies secured a market for the budding manufacturers, and, through the monopoly of the market, and increased accumulation. The treasures captured outside Europe by undisguised looting, enslavement, and murder, floated back to the mother-country and were there turned into capital. Holland, which first fully developed the colonial system, in 1648 stood already in the acme of its commercial greatness.

Quoting Gulich, Marx continues that:

It was in almost exclusive possession of the East Indian trade and the commerce between the south-east and north-west of Europe. Its fisheries, marine, manufactures, surpassed those of any other country. The total capital of the Republic was probably more important than that of all the rest of Europe put together.

Marx shows that:

Gulich forgets to add that by 1648, the people of Holland were more over-worked, and more brutally oppressed than those of all the rest of Europe put together.[6]

The oppression and exploitation of the Dutch labouring classes in a larger society within which the dominant classes were avidly accumulating capital negatively affected the prosperity of even the greater proportion of the petty bourgeoisie. Van Ravesteyn informs that during the first quarter of the 17th century, there developed in Amsterdam a mass of petty bourgeoisie, members of guilds who although throughout the period continuously received higher financial rewards; in real terms, relative to the expanding capital of the higher bourgeoisie, the petty bourgeoisie economically regressed, and in a material sense their economic position was more or less proletarian.[7] The poor conditions of the masses was not eliminated by the century-long prosperity of the Golden Age. Indeed, out of 41,561 households at Amsterdam in 1747, it has been estimated that some 19,000 were actually living in really squalid back premises, cellars and basements. Until the end of the 17th century, most houses in the rural areas and many in the towns were built of wood and clay. Stone or brick homes were a rarity for all except the rich.[8]

Long before the Dutch West India Company became established on the Gold Coast, in fact, individual Dutch merchants had been sporadically trading along the coast since the closing years of the 16th century. These were the elements who supported the original ideas about establishing the West India Company. For a time, mainly during the 12 years truce which lasted until 1609, they undertook individual trading ventures to the Guinea Coast. One of these regent-oligarchs, the Zeelander, Balthasar de Moucheron, is reputed to have heavily invested in these trading adventures to Guinea and was the prime mover of the unsuccessful attempt to take Elmina Castle from the Portuguese in 1596. It has been estimated that during the closing years of the 16th century and the first few years of the 17th, over 10,000 sailors and a total of about 120 ships undertook trading voyages to the Guinea Coast. It was during this period that rich merchants, ship owners and captains principally in places like Middleburg, Dordrecht, Rotterdam and Amsterdam started organizing rival co-operative companies to pursue more effectively the trade with Guinea.[9] The creators of the Dutch West India Company were firm and dogmatic Calvinists, convinced and resolved on a policy of destruction of the Spanish empire.

The organization and structure of the West India Company (WIC), which received its charter from the States-General on 3rd June, 1621, was essentially modelled in a variety of ways on that of the older VOC (Dutch East India Company), although it should be indicated that the offensive role of the WIC in the long war of attrition against the

Spanish American empire was emphasized from the start of its life. The WIC, was given a monopoly of all Dutch trade and commerce with the Americas and West Africa. Furthermore, it was granted state authority to freely bear the Dutch flag and to make war and peace with the indigenous peoples and powers, to develop and maintain naval and land forces, and to formulate, and exercise judicial and administrative functions in those regions as it saw fit and necessary. The WIC, though founded largely with the immediate political aim of eliminating Spain from America and the silver of Mexico and Peru, actually focussed for profits on the sugar of Portuguese Brazil, and on the gold, ivory, and slaves of Portuguese West Africa. It was composed of five regional chambers — Amsterdam, Zeeland (Middleburg), The Mass (Rotterdam), North-Quarter, and Groningen with Friesland. The WIC counterpart to the *Heeren XVII* was a central board or governing body of the *Heeren XIX*. The WIC needed a considerably longer time to raise its working capital than the VOC had done. But the amount which was ultimately raised was substantially larger, being just over seven million florins. The formation of a West India Company was suggested much earlier in the 17th century, but was held up by the twelve-year truce between Spain and the Dutch republic in 1609. On the whole, of all the European chartered companies of the 17th and 18th centuries, the WIC was the most successful. During the whole course of its history (1621-1791) it was very actively involved with trading on the Guinea Coast.

In spite of the protracted and costly war with Spain, during the 17th century the Dutch and other European powers maintained a steady supply of slaves from Africa, mainly the West Coast, to the New World. This trade in Africans developed throughout the Golden Age of the Netherlands to be the essential source of prosperity and wealth of the Dutch West India Company. After Spain signed for peace in 1648, Dutch operations with respect to slave trading became more intensive and led Europe in this trade until the early decades of the 18th century when during the War of Spanish Succession (1701-1713) the Dutch lost the contract (*Asiento*) for slave deliveries to the English. In the course of the ocean-crossing of the heavily overcrowded ships which plied the Atlantic with their human cargo; in what was known as the "middle passage" at least 25% of the slaves lost their lives. The procurement of the *Asiento* by the English in 1713 gave them the right until 1743 to export to Spanish America alone, 4800 Africans per year.[10]

The notorious "middle passage" has been given vivid description.

> The negroes were chained to each other hand and foot, and stowed so close that they were not allowed above a foot and half for each in breadth. Thus rammed together like herrings in a barrel, they contracted putrid and fatal disorders; so that they who came to inspect them in a morning had occasionally to pick dead slaves out of their rows, and to unchain their carcasses from the bodies of their wretched fellow-sufferers to whom they had been fastened.[11]

The glory of the Dutch Golden Age was on the wane by the end of the 17th century. The Netherlands still enjoyed considerable prosperity but relative to the other European contemporary powers, the Dutch pre-eminence of the preceding century was in decline. English and French mercantilism irreversibly cut the lead of the Dutch in trade and commerce. The English were the first to pose a real threat and challenge to the Dutch. The Anglo-Dutch wars of the 17th century contributed in part to the weakening of Dutch control over international trade. In 1651, the Rump in Cromwellian England passed the Navigation Act which legislated that all goods imported into England should be brought either by English ships or ships of the country of origin of the imports. This piece of legislation was not only meant to carve out a niche and place for England in the overseas trade. It was particularly directed at depriving the Dutch of some of the carrying trade they had hitherto controlled. A French assessment of the size of the Dutch mercantile marine in the 1660s suggested that the Dutch mercantile fleet was about twice the size of those of England and France combined. A.C. Carter has argued that the treaty of Breda in, 1667 and its sequel appeared to bring the Dutch advantages, there were also some ill-effects of the war. Among these was the transfer during its course of large numbers of Dutch flyboats to the English mercantile marine as prizes. As the English were already beginning to impair the Dutch lead in the field of Europe's carrying trade, this seriously unbalanced the previous equation between the two fleets. Although the Dutch could and did still build ships quickly, the English merchant marine became stronger during and after the war than it had been previously, in spite of its own considerable losses and in spite of the poverty of the English crown. Indeed it is arguable that the end of the second Anglo-Dutch war marks the downturn of the Republic's prosperity, and that thereafter, with threat to its security, and conditions becoming less favourable to its trade, the long drawn-out process of decline got under way.[12]

Indeed it has been pointed out that during the naval wars attendant on the War of the League of Augsburg (1689-1697) and the War of Spanish Succession 1701-1713, in which wars the English and Dutch were allies, it was the English navy which bore the brunt of the seaborne battles, and by the close of the wars the Dutch were hardpressed to put a dozen ships of the line to sea.[13]

The French in many ways matched the English in attempting to halt Dutch international trading power. In the France of Louis XIV, their economic brain Colbert introduced high tariffs on imports in the effort to curb the influence of the Dutch. Trading monopoly companies were established to close the French colonial trade to the Dutch. Cardinal Richelieu had made active attempts to build a strong fleet. It was however again Colbert who really created the French fleet capable of holding its own against allcomers. Williams informs us that by the time of Colbert's death in 1683 the French navy was equal to the combined strengths of the English and Dutch fleets.[14]

For centuries before Capitein's era, there had always been

some Africans in European society. Generally within the European class structures, they had very inferior positions being either slaves or former slaves. A few like William Amo (1703-1756) also from the Gold Coast, achieved elevated social positions in European society in contrast to the low social positions of most other blacks.[15] In any case, blacks were within European society very much objects of curiosity. The "expansion of Europe" and the Atlantic slave era saw indirectly, the rapid introduction of more Africans into Europe. Although little authoritative or substantial historical sources on Africans in the Netherlands during Capitein's lifetime exist, in the case of Britain, it is known that Henry VII employed a black trumpeter in 1508 for 24 pounds per year. Many black soldiers, drummers, actors, doctors, dentists, and servants were part of British life and society during the 16th and 17th centuries. In 1601, Elizabeth I issued an edict decrying the large numbers of "Negroes and blackamoors" in England and recommended their deportation. During the 17th and 18th centuries black servants became rather popular. A particularly well-known one was Francis Barber, Dr. Johnson's servant who is reputed to have helped Boswell to write the latter's biography of Johnson. During the 17th century the black population in Britain increased. Many of them lived as the dregs of society carrying on a marginal existence in the twilight scene of the underworld and dockside London. Those blacks who were more privileged worked as flunkeys, coachmen, footmen and the like. Some Africans of aristocratic birth had elevated positions in the court-life of the Stuarts, as the diaries of Pepys and Evelyn reveal.[16]

During Capitein's time some blacks in Britain organized themselves into secret societies for their protection and encouraged others to escape their bondage. During the 18th century blacks in London numbered between 14-20,000 in a city of 750,000. In 1731 the Lord Mayor of London published a proclamation that no negro apprentices should be employed.[17] Blacks were also not unknown in court circles in 18th century Germany. The presence of negroes in European society did not necessarily easily dispel cockeyed views about black humanity. Blacks were more often than not either regarded with curiosity and paternalism or utter disdain : either Rousseau's noble savage, Defoe's Robinson Crusoe, Aphra Behn's Oroonoko, or the savages Defoe's Captain Singleton encountered on his remarkable journey across "unexplored" Africa. Kiernan writes that,

> In the eighteenth century there were believed to be several thousands in London, and slaves were advertised and rewards offered for absconders until slavery on British soil was ended by the Mansfield judgement of 1772. An aura of servitude clung to Africans as a race, finding such expression as the Amsterdam inn-sign on which a Negro in chains crouched at the feet of a pipe-smoking young white merchant. It took a softened, stylized form in the vogue, which has left many quaint memorials in Dresden China, of African flunkeys or page-boys in great houses. A multitude of black faces may at times, repel white people (and equally the converse), but a black face here and there was attractively exotic, and set off the powdered hair and satin gowns of the company as the ladies' patches did their cheeks. An urbanized aristocracy wants its servants very distinctly marked off from it, as a different species of humanity, and an African in European finery met this requirement perfectly. In 1748 a Lieutenant Bemish brought home a black boy, 'a good-natured child, about ten years old', to present to Admiral Boscawen's lady, who felt she could not civily decline, especially as the boy had been handsomely rigged out in her livery.[18]

Capitein indeed, was educated in Europe at a time when the most absurd prejudices about the African was in common currency. Prejudice thrives on ignorance, and one tends to associate vulgar ignorance with uneducated social types. Unfortunately, some of the scholarly types of the age entertained and vocalised the most shocking opinions. Daniel Defoe's *Captain Singleton* of 1720, portrayed the first Africans his castaways found among themselves as,

> an ignorant, ravenous, brutish sort of people, even worse than the natives of any other country that we had seen;[19]

It was within this climate of opinion in Europe of the early 18th century that Capitein saw his formative years.

The Netherlands Capitein saw was a society which was highly stratified. People were conscious of their class positions and social status. One of the interesting peculiarities of western expansion and colonialism has been that, generally throughout the European colonial empire, the colonialists among themselves have tended to exaggerate their social and cultural mores. Class gradations and distinctions tended to be over-emphasized. Within the structure of the overseas wings of the Dutch West India Company, hierarchical differentiations were rigidly and meticulously maintained, and the fine gradations of precedence and rank were faithfully followed. This tended to exacerbate social tensions and conflicts, and an African, generally disparaged by Europeans, who found himself actively caught up in the class and rank conflicts of Europeans must have had a particularly rough time.

Durions and distinctions tended to be over-emphasized. Within the structure of the overseas wings of the Dutch West India Company, hierarchical differentiations were rigidly and meticulously maintained, and the fine gradations of precedence and rank were faithfully followed. This tended to exacerbate social tensions and conflicts, and an African, generally disparaged by Europeans, who finds himself actively caught up in the class and rank conflicts of Europeans must have had a particularly rough time.

During the early 18th century, Europeans in the Gold Coast, were almost all either individual traders or elements in the pay of the European trading companies. They were in Africa solely to make money by fair or foul means, for, as

Bosman admitted:

> I don't believe that those who can live on their
> means in Holland, will ever come to such a
> country as this.[20]

Barbot's comments in this respect are even more direct
and biting. He wrote that:

> The great concern of the Dutch on this Coast, as
> well as of all other Europeans settled or trading
> there, is the gold, and not the welfare of those
> souls.[21]

K. Ratelband's view is that it was neither the will to
conquer, the spirit of adventure, nor indeed an evangelical
zeal which motivated the Dutch in Guinea. The object of
their endeavours was, the pursuit of gain.[22]

Writing in 1602 De Marees' language and opinion on the
Dutch in Guinea is even more florid;

> gold is their god.[23]

This is not surprising for as has recently been pointed out,
during the early 17th century in the United Netherlands:

> practically all gold coins in the republic were
> made out of Guinea gold.[24]

The schematic structure of positions and relations among
the Europeans working in Elmina for the Dutch West India
Company at the beginning of the 18th century has been
provided by Bosman. The picture is as follows:

The Director-General
The Preacher, (always next to the Director)
The Fiscal
The Chief Factor

Two or three Chief-Factors besides
Seven or eight Factors
Nine or ten Sub-Factors
Eighteen or twenty Assistants

> The number of these varies daily; so that there are sometimes more, and several times less of each.

A Ware-house Keeper
Accountant or Book-keeper General
Under Book-keeper
Accountant or Book-keeper to the Garrison
Clerk of the Church
An Auditor or Informer.[25]

Apart from these people ultimate control and regulation of affairs falling within the interest sphere of the Dutch West India Company along the whole of the Gold Coast, was theoretically taken care of by another more high-powered body. Again Bosman explains:

> The Government or Direction of the Coast is principally vested in the Director-General as the Supreme ruler; from whom all Governors of the out-forts receive their commands; and subordinate to whom they are obliged to act, they not being empowered to transact any important affairs without his knowledge and entire consent: But difficult affairs, or those of greater importance, are cognizable to, and out to be laid before the assembly of Counsellors, or Council composed of, viz.
> The Director-General
> The Fiscal, in other things besides Criminal cases
> The Chief-Factors
> The Ensign or Banner-Bearer, and sometimes
> The Accountant-General.[26]

Feinberg makes useful elaborations to the various roles and ranks. In terms of the commercial activities of the West India Company, the *Opperkoopman or Opperkommis* (chief factor), in the 18th century Guinea coastal society, was second to the Director-General. In case of the death of the Director-

General he assumed the latter's position. The chief factor could be stationed at Elmina but more often he was commandant of another important fort such as St. Sebastian at Shama, or St. Anthony at Axim. The factor or *Commis* was usually a commandant of a minor fort. Some were also clerks and book-keepers in the Elmina administration. The sub-factors or *Onder-Commisen* were in-charge generally of receiving and collecting gold, and Assistants were the lowest ranking administrative personnel. There were also artificers who operated as coopers, blacksmiths, carpenters, bricklayers, locksmiths and coppersmiths. These artificers were assisted by company slaves (*Trainsslaven*) who sometimes picked up the skills of their immediate masters. These slaves owned and used by the West India Company were several hundred strong during the 18th century; they were of both sexes and of all ages. The company slaves in Elmina lived in a separate quarter of the town, and were given *kostgeld* or pocket money varying between one-half engel every two months to three engels every two months.[27]

Interestingly, we are informed that the pastors' position was theoretically considered to be of great importance and distinction. This was Capitein's historical position, and it must have attracted the indignation and jealousy of some of the other Europeans, particularly the lower class types; apart from everything, also because the position was being occupied by a blackamoor. Obviously, the privileges were considerable, for as Bosman writes:

> Having run through our Temporal State, we now come to our spiritual preferments; which are but two, the first a Minister, with a salary of one hundred, the second a Clerk, with that of twenty Guilders per month; besides which, the first hath ten Guilders per month allowed for a servant, and a place at the Governor's table. What do you think, Sir? Don't we pay our clergyman pretty well? I'll assure you, if you think we live licentious lives, you are in the wrong, for, we are very religious; we are obliged to go to church every day, or forfeiture of twenty five Styvers, except on

Sundays and Thursdays, when the forfeiture for omission is doubled: But I know you will reply, this is a forced service of God, and consequently not always accompanied with the most sincere intentions: And to confess the truth; it is not much better: for, were not the restraints laid upon us, some would rather pay a visit elsewhere than to the church.[28]

It is thus, quite clear that the regulations stipulated a fairly rigorous religious life. The practice was, however, often different. For Capitein experienced great difficulty in getting the support of the castle community for his religious activities.[29] Also, some of the pastors were not always exemplar enough, as was the case of Capitein's predecessor, Isaac Ketelanus.[30] Of course, when the religious leader himself becomes undisciplined, it is difficult to expect the community to be regular and diligent in their religious practices. All the available evidence indicates that Capitein for his part, pursued his duties conscientiously, in the early years.

One of the long-standing and outstanding mistakes in the study of African societies, has been the often argued myth of classlessness of African societies in the past and present.[31] Some observers have shifted former positions of denial and come to accept the existence of classes in contemporary Africa. However, the entrenched character of the anti-historical school is so firmly rooted that it dies hard and thus although today, more than yesterday, many would accept the existence of classes in Africa, a considerable proportion of scientists would still deny their existence in the pre-colonial period. Even though enough evidence exists to substantiate the existence of classes in the pre-colonial period.

It is not difficult to explain that, of course, so long as the existence of classes in the past, but particularly the present is disputed, the politics of class struggle is implicitly dismissed. Indeed in effect, one must admit that the whole ideology of classlessness, protects class rule.

The African settlements in the immediate neighbourhood of the European forts were closely linked in their economic and social life to the European powers which ran these forts. Although the extent of European influence on the African settlements differed from place to place and from time to time. In some places, the European power or powers could and did extract tolls from the African inhabitants. During the late 17th and early 18th centuries, the Dutch who controlled Fort Nassau had such powers.

> The Village Mouree lying under it, is not so large as Elmina, but more populous; the greatest part of its inhabitants are fisher-men, who go out every morning four or five hundred canoes to fish, and upon their return are obliged to pay the fifth fish as toll to our factor, who governs this town. This sort of toll we yet reserve at three places besides, viz. at Axim, Shama and Elmina by reason that we have conquered these places, though I dare not affirm that of Mouree. No other Europeans have this peculiar prerogative, nor do any of them exercise such a sovereign authority over their Negro subjects as we; which is indeed chiefly their own fault, and by their means we have also lost some of our former power.[32]

Probably the degree of taxation in the form of tolls in kind (fish) varied considerably from place to place. Barbot indicates that the rate of toll extraction in Axim differed from Mouree. His words are that,

> the fishermen pay the Dutch factor the eighth part of all the fish they take, which is pretty considerable, there being many of them at Axim.[33]

Feinberg's researches on this aspect of Dutch-Elminan relations reveal that in the 17th century the toll was 20 per cent of the catch. However, during the 18th century, this increased to about 25 per cent. Schematically, the toll was as follows:[34]

1 Fish — No toll

```
 2 Fish — Toll: half fish
 3 Fish — Toll: The body of one fish
 4 Fish — Toll: One fish
 5 Fish — Toll: One fish
 6 Fish — Toll: One and one-half fish
 7 Fish — Toll: One fish and the body of another
 8 Fish — Toll: Two fish
 9 Fish — Toll: Two fish
10 Fish — Toll: Two and one-half fish
```

This sort of taxation was an adaptation from the indigenous practice common to the coastal Fanti under which system, the chief appropriated 25 per cent of fish caught by fishermen in his domain. Thus in addition to tolls paid to the chief also in those coastal towns where the Dutch maintained a fortified presence, tolls were also paid to the Dutch. Feinberg also informs us that:

> The Elmina leaders, at one time received a toll or custom on slaves traded in the castle. The origins of this payment are unknown, but it was not being paid in 1739, when the Elminans made a request for its resumption. A toll may also have been received on ships coming into the harbour, but the evidence for this is indirect. In 1642, the Dutch agreed to pay the Axim Caboceers one ounce of gold for each new ship coming from the Fatherland with cargo for the Gold Coast.[35]

Dutch overlordship of Elmina society was expressed also in juridical prerogatives for the maintenance of law and order in the town. Penalties existed for breaches of the peace and major crimes such as theft, arson and murder. The Dutch authorities reserved the right of incarcerating culprits. They could imprison even important Africans using them as hostages in order to gain leverage in negotiations. To underwrite and enforce their power, the Dutch on occasions used force by firing on the town. They could simply close the Benya River and thereby prevent the fishermen from going out to fish. Existing evidence however suggests that by and large during the 18th century, the Dutch and Elminans came to prolonged conflict once, 1739-1740, two years before Capitein arrived on the coast.

Although placed squarely in Fantiland the Elminas in mythology, history and tradition regard themselves as distinct from the Fanti. In actual fact this distinction is fairly marginal, for in essence their social structure and culture shares the overwhelming body of attributes which characterize the Akan people of the area. These similarities did not however prevent conflicts between the various feudalities in the region.

As Amissah has argued, the 17th century coastal Fante possessed an elaborate hierarchized structure.[36] Of course, this structure originated from long before that time. Within the then existing feudal structure, gradations of aristocratic rank and office existed. The foremost being the king, chieftain, or village head. The aristocrats (*Adehye*) were generally called *Brenipono or Brempon* (in Twi *Obarima*). This class was generally excluded from agricultural labour, being concerned mainly with military, judicial, and administrative functions. They could be distinguished from their lesser compatriots by the dresses and often luxurious life style and the following or train they commanded in public.[37] Religious priests formed a privileged group being also often exempted from productive labour. They were variously known as *Abossum Fo*, *Nkomfo* or *Essuman Fo*. Traditional traders were known as *Batafo*. It is useful to distinguish these traders from the newer type of traders thrown up largely as a result of trade with the Europeans along the coast. This new group often derived from the middle and lower aristocracy. Although as time went on probably the distinction between the older traditional type of traders and the newer, more western engendered trading group, tended to disappear. The trading African nobility were often called *Grandees* (Prominents). They generally combined their aristocratic and trading activities and some of them became *Caboceers*, or sometimes linguists for the trading companies. Smith defines a *Caboceroe* as:

> the Master of a Town, or Head of a Clan, who in
> Military Affairs, acts as General, and in Civil as a

Judge, making up all Pallavers, or deciding all Controversies among the poorer Sort.[38]

Also Priestley[39] adds that, actually the title *Caboceer* is a later corruption of the older Portuguese term *Caboceiro*, meaning captain. The version *Caboceer* must be a Dutch rendering of the Portuguese. Bosman described them as,

> civil fathers, whose province is only to take care of the welfare of the city, or village, and to appease any tumult,

and Sarbah, in his time, adds that:

> The foreign term *Caboceer* has fallen into disuse, and the ordinary term *Omanfu* is not so often used in these days as *Penyin*, *Penyinfu*. The persons holding this office are commonly limited in number, and are elected thereto.[40]

Most of the Caboceers were regarded as Grandees, i.e. prominents. They were those who mattered in decision-making about important matters concerning the community, and some like John Conny, John Kabes, Thomas Osiat, Abbocon, John Curantee, and Brempong Kojo, featured interestingly in the 17th and 18th century histories of the Gold Coast.[41] However, as Bosman explains, the Caboceers were in origin not always aristocrats. Bosman points out that:

> The Principal Men or Caboceros are commonly limited to a set number; but some of them dying and the vacancies not filling, when upon assembling together they find their number too small, they choose out of the Commonalty Persons well advanced in Years to complete their number (for young men are seldom admitted into this Honourable Assembly) who, electing brethren by a present of a cow and some drink; after which they are lawfully admitted and confirmed. The

custom of Axim obliges the candidate for this dignity to be a native of that country living at Axim, at least keeping a house there, inhabited by one of his wives, or some of his family, and sometimes residing there himself; which is somewhat like our being obliged to keep fire and light to preserve our right of citizens in Holland.

If there be one alone, or several, he or they are all brought to our fort and presented to our factor, with a request that they may be admitted into their society; who, if he hath nothing to object against him, administers an Oath to him on the Bible, obliging him to be and remain true to the Netherlanders, and to aid and assist them to the utmost of his power against all their enemies whatsoever, whether Europeans or Negroes, and deport himself on all occasions as a Loyal Subject: after which he takes an Oath, not unlike the former, respecting his own Nation; both which Oaths are confirmed by an imprecation . . . . This done, the factor having registered his name, acknowledges him a member of their assembly, and admits him to all the rights, privileges and advantages appendant thereto; and having made the due presents to his brethren, he is a Caboceer during his life. In other places on the coast, the Election of a Caboceer is somewhat different; but it being so well regulated at Axim, I shall content myself with describing that only.[42]

In a sense the Caboceers can be considered to have been some of the earliest *Comprador* types in the coastal economic structure. They worked very closely with the European factors and other traders along the coast, and together with the factors, even extracted money fines from culprits and infringers of the coastal legal code which together with the European factors, they upheld. In this sense, they operated also as magistrates or judges. Barbot, with reference to Axim noted that:

For example, if a Black be fined a hundred crowns for any crime, the factor's fee amount to two thirds, and the assembly of Caboceiros has the other third; but in cases of murder or robbery, or compelling them to pay debts, three fourths of the whole are the plaintiff's, and the other fourth is for the factor and the Caboceiros; the former taking two thirds thereof, and the latter one.[43]

The soldiery consisted mostly of all able-bodied men under the king, however, there was a smaller group of professional armed retainers of the king or chieftain: this group was partly supported by the state. A wider generalized picture as to the source of African soldiers has been given; by Bosman. He writes that:

> If I have before talk'd of Negroes who followed the Wars, you must not from thence infer that they make that their whole employment: No, it is but one part, I assure you; and all the Negroes in general are Soldiers as long as the War continues, if at least they are but able to buy Arms, or their Masters bestow any on them; and the War ended each Man applies himself to the Exercise of his particular Calling: But if there happens to be any of such a turbulent Nature that they cannot live out of the Camp, they go to serve in the Neighbouring Wars; and these are in a stricter sense called Soldiers. Amongst the Fishermen there are very few Soldiers; for they, living upon the Shore and under our Protection, are not frequently attack'd by Enemies; and therefore, are seldom furnished with Arms.[44]

There were also a wide variety of craftsmen and artisans, musicians and jesters. These latter were mainly commoners who were not under bondage. By the middle of the 18th century, a great part of the labourers on land were slaves *Donkorfo*. These were mainly war-captives, or people received as tribute or bondsmen usually from elsewhere. In Capitein's time these were the main social groupings among many of the coastal Fante. These class and rank differentiations can be filled in with Bosman's scheme of classification. Although, admittedly his scheme is not based on a scientific definition of class or rank, it indicates the existence of a class structure. He writes that:

> I have observed five Degrees of men amongst the Negroes; the first of which are their Kings or Captains, for the Word is here Synonymous. The second, their Cabocero's of Chief Men; which reducing to our manner of Expression, we should be apt to call them Civil Fathers; whose Province is only to take care of the Welfare of the City or Village, and to appease any Tumult. The third sort are those who have acquired a great Reputation by their Riches, either devolved on them by Inheritance of gotten by Trade. And these are the Persons which some Authors have represented as Noblemen; but whether they are in the right or not, shall hereafter plainly appear. The fourth are the common People employed in the Tillage of Wines, Agriculture and Fishing. The fifth and the last are the Slaves, either sold by their Relations, taken in War, or come so by Poverty.[45]

Class and rank differentiations were also manifested in the social life and expression of the people. Wealthy people wore large clothes, of three to four ells in size (one ell is 27 inches) and made of silk, velvet, or perpetuana although alternatively he may wear what Bosman describes as "a sort of paan ... made of fifty sorts of stuff." Caboceers generally wore not only a good cloth, but also a cap of animal skin, and a commoner such as a fisherman, wore a cloth of only one or two ells. The size of a man's house was also an indicator to his social position. Most of the houses were of mud and clay, but a wealthy man's house may be two storeys high, near the market, and would be separated from the dwelling of fisherfolk.[46]

Throughout the 18th century, the class basis of Gold Coast society became even more firmly entrenched, however in response to the penetration of West European mercantile capitalism, in African society, capitalist induced elements appeared to grow more and eat into the fabric of the old feudal structure, with its older slave economic base. The class of petty traders expanded, also the early African proletariat created in response to the effects of western capitalism on the coast continued to increase. The history of this latter class along the Gold Coast is interesting.

Writing about West Africa in 1744, when Capitein was in Elmina, William Smith clarifies that:

> A *Grometta* is a black free-man who hires himself by the week, to work for any one, but chiefly for white men, by whom many are here employed.[47]

This was in the mid-eighteenth century. Actually the term *Grometta* is of Portuguese origin, and dates from the period of Portuguese dominance on the West African coast. This strongly indicates that the beginning of an African proletariat along the coast developed in response to the influence of early Portuguese capitalism in West Africa. Evidence shows that originally, the term applied to a type of Portuguese crew. Later it came to apply also to Africans in wage employment. Boxer tells us that:

> A *carrack* (type of early Portuguese ship) in the *Carreira* (a round voyage between Portugal and India in the days of sail) was supposed to be crewed by about 120 or 130 foremast hands, equally divided between able (and ordinary) seamen and *grumetes* (grummets). These latter, were apprentice seamen, not necessarily boys, though most of them were usually in their teens. They did all the hardest work on board, and they slept on the deck at the waist between the

mainmast and the foremast. Many of them had never been in a ship till they left Lisbon for Goa, and Martin Alfonso de Sousa observed of this type: "Let nobody tell you that when they arrive they are already sailors. This is the biggest lie in the world, for they are vagabonds who have never been to sea; and in order to become a sailor it is necessary to serve for many years as a grummet. And, I assure you that these are the ones who desert to the Muslims here . . . . for they have no sense of duty, and as soon as they lack a farthing of their wages, off they go".[48]

Another observer, a companion of Sieur André Brüe, a Frenchman who was, for many years Director-General of the French Sanaga (Senegal) Company at Fort. St. Louis, writing in 1701 notes that in the Portuguese fort at Bissao, of the Garrison,

> which was or ought to have consisted of 15 *Gromettas*; or hired Blacks. Only the Governor, his Lieutenant, and Alsere (or Ensign) were whites; the Sergeant being an old black Creolian of St. Jago.[49]

In a footnote, the writer informs us further that the term *Gromettas* is,

> so written, according to the Portuguese, by Barbot and Atkins, but in Labat, Gourmet, they are the same with those called *Laptots*, at the Sanaga and Gambra.

Elmina is situated on one of the most naturally beautiful stretches of coast along the Gulf of Guinea. The present main inhabitants were originally part of the old Akan migrants who came to the coast from the far interior Techiman during the 13th century. Till today, their contacts with Techiman have been maintained, and on special occasions such as royal funerals, emissaries come down from Techiman for the relevant ceremonies.

Along this part of the West African coast, Elmina was the first place Europeans made a foothold. These were the Portuguese who first touched Edina (Elmina) in 1471. Some historians have made largely unsubstantiated and very doubtful claims that in fact, the European presence here, dates from an earlier period; that the French were there already in the 14th century.[50]

The Portuguese very quickly appreciated the tremendous possibilities for trade in the area. They were particularly impressed by the fact that there was a great amount of gold available in the area which was worn and displayed in quantity and quality by the feudal aristocrats and their satraps. It was because of this apparent availability of gold that the Portuguese gave the name Elmina (The Mine) to the whole stretch of coast.[51] Other Europeans were hot on the heels of the Portuguese. For this reason in 1480, King John II of Portugal approved the establishment of a permanent trading post along the Gold Coast. They chose the most naturally favourable point to establish their post, St. George d'Elmina. This started on the 21st of January, 1482. The whole project was under the supervision of Don Diego da Azambuja who had under his command 600 men, including 100 carpenters and 100 masons plus other necessary building materials. Four years later in 1486, the Portuguese King conferred the status of a city on Elmina. The Portuguese Governor or "Captain-General" of the castle represented the Portuguese King, and held all the relevant powers (civil and military) in Elmina on behalf of the King, and it was from this castle that the first systematic Portuguese exportation of slaves took place.[52] In *The Age of Reconnaissance*, J.H. Parry points out that, the Portuguese trade through Elmina was chiefly in gold, slaves and pepper, with sidelines in ivory, gum, wax, palm oil, occasional ostrich eggs and similar curiosities. The principal exports however were cloth and hardware. Locally the trade was run by individual merchants and firms holding licenses granted by the crown, which ultimately held the monopoly for the trade. The crown reserved the right to monopolize the purchase of some commodities on arrival in Portugal. The ivory trade was exclusively reserved under the Gomes lease; this later was changed. Trade in pepper was a royal prerogative. Under the radius of the shadow of the Portuguese guns, the garrison maintained de facto control of the city.[53] The Dutch were the first European power to challenge Portuguese power in Elmina. In 1596, they undertook their first attack of the Portuguese post. In 1612, the Dutch built a fort at Mouri, 12 miles east of Elmina. The Dutch finally ousted the Portuguese in 1637, and remained in control of the castle until 1869, when they transferred it to the British.

It is clear from available evidence that Elmina town had for a long time before Capitein's period, been subjected to European rule. Barbot writing, on the basis of observations made probably during the 1680s indicated that:

> The town is divided into three distinct parts, as if there were three large villages near one another; each part of ward is governed by its effective *Braffo*; which *Braffo* or governor is assisted by a Caboceiro, and some other inferior officers, who administer justice, and have charge of the political state: And these, all together, compose the regency of this little republic, ever since the Portuguese made it independent of the Kings of Commendo and of Fetu, who formerly were masters of it by equal halves. This happened some few years before the Dutch conquer'd the castle of Mina from the Portuguese .... The affairs of the republic were formerly debated in the house of the *Braffo* of one of the wards one time, and next, in that of another *Braffo* alternatively; and the deliberations or elections made there, were carried to the Dutch general to approve of them: If he did not, they were to debate matters again in another assembly, till what was transacted was consented to by that general; which also was the method they were liable to when under the protection of

the Portuguese.[54]

Thus, in addition to the powers and rights to tax in kind the inhabitants of these coastal towns which had European forts (e.g. Axim, Mouree, Elmina, Shama), the European powers' operations on the coast during the 17th and 18th centuries also regulated and controlled legal aspects of the life of these coastal Africans, and maintained standing armies to enforce their wishes. In effect, the conditions and characteristics of government which later on, in the late 19th century became widely accepted as colonialism in the sense that it is understood today, in actual fact, started and were created in albeit rudimentary form long before Europeans achieved *de jure* colonial control of this part of Africa. Thus, the emergence of colonialism in the Gold Coast was not an abrupt phenomenon. It emerged first as a steadily expanding and deepening *de facto* control of stretches of the African coast long before the era of capitalist imperialism when the colonial phenomenon in this part of Africa assumed *de jure* properties. Daaku has, in fact, drawn attention to the similarities in the structure of European presence on the West African coast, during the 17th and the 19th centuries.[55] It is important, however, to conceive the character of European presence in the 17th and 18th centuries in its proper perspective. During the 17th and 18th centuries, these coastal enclaves with fortified European presence were in a sense largely coastal trading principalities which although had close historical, economic, and social connections with the hinterland, were all the same politico-economic structures developing rapidly in response to the stimulus of mercantile capitalist commodity trade. This trade tended to orient the economies of these coastal principalities out of Africa into an emergent world commodity market dominated and regulated from western Europe. Away from the coast, the socio-economic structures of these hinterland societies tended relatively to maintain more conservatively their natural economic character; the level of commodity production and trade was relatively lower, and the further northwards one went, the more the direction of trade also

91

pointed northwards across the Western Sudan. However, by the late 17th and early 18th centuries, even for many of the groups in the hinterland of present-day Ghana, the trade with the coastal principalities and their European controllers was steadily affecting the internal dynamics of these relatively predominant natural economies and catalysing changes in the forces and relations of production. The increased availability of firearms intensified the resolution of feudal conflicts in frequent wars. As Daaku explains, basing his argument on Bosman and other 17th century writers,

> the Europeans did not, like the Spanish in the New World, control the sources of 'the Gold' or 'the slaves'. It was, therefore, necessary that those who controlled the sources of the commodities should be induced to trade with them. States like Denkyira, Akwamu, Asante, and Akyem, which became powerful in the course of the 17th century, could easily disorganize trade. It was, therefore, as important, if not more so, to seek their goodwill as it was to be on good terms with the coastal states.[56]

During the early 18th century, the dominant power in the hinterland area was Akwamu. Originally a small state in the Agona area, it grew through conquest and incorporation eastwards to the area directly north of Accra. Between 1677 and 1681 the Akwamu took Accra, in 1688 Agona was subdued, and by the beginning of the 18th century the Akwamu were on the banks of the Volta. Through conquest and subjugation their jurisdiction eastwards stretched as far as Ouidah. This latter remained under Akwamu sway until 1727 when Ouidah was taken by Dahomey. Fage underlines the spectacularity of Akwamu expansion by indicating that at the height of its power, the Akwamu took Christiansborg Castle from the Danes and later sold it back to them.[57] The Akwamu empire did not last long, and after the defeat by Akim in 1730, the empire fell apart. At the time Capitein came to Elmina, Ashanti power had superceded the

Akwamu. In size, extent and power it eclipsed whatever empires had preceded it in the immediate area. Ashanti power emerged during the last stages of the 17th century. In 1700 it defeated the Denkyira and the rapid expansion of Ashanti continued throughout the 18th century, first in alliance with Akwamu, later Ashanti outstripped Akwamu influence. The founders of Ashanti power were Osei Tutu and his friend Okomfo Anokye. It was however Opoku Ware (1720-1750) who pushed the frontiers of Ashanti outwards. In 1742 the year Capitein arrived in Elmina, the Ashanti armies fought the Akim. The Akim were defeated and the Ashanti soon proceeded southwards towards Accra. After the defeat of the Akim, Ashanti dominance was consolidated in the hinterland of the Gold Coast: Parts of Akim and Kwawu were annexed and overlordship was reinforced in Sefwi, Assin, Denkyira, Aowin, Akuapim and Twifo. The Dutch and the Danes on the coast, through skillful diplomacy, bribery, tribute, and rents, were able generally to hold their own and maintain good relations with the emergent Ashanti empire.[58]

Notes

CHAPTER V

1. Jan Romein is probably the most significant Dutch historian so far this century. This phrase is in fact the title of his study of Dutch history, *De lage landen by de zee.*

2. See Pieter Geyl's short informative essay: The National State and the Writers of Netherlands History. In *Debates with Historians* (by the same author). London. 1967 edition.

3. J. Goudsblom. *Dutch Society.* New York. 1967. p. 16.

4. Defoe. A Plan of the English Commerce 1728. Quoted here from C.H. Wilson. The Economic Decline of the Netherlands.In E.M. Carus-Wilson (ed.) Vol. I. - *Essays in Economic History,* London, 1954 (1961 edition), p. 225.

5. C.H. Wilson. op cit.

6. Karl Marx: *Capital.* Part 8. chapter 31.

7. See W. van Ravensteyn, Jr. *Onderzoekingen over de economischen social outwikkeling van Amsterdam gedurende de 16 de en het eerste kwart der 17de eeuw.* Amsterdam. 1906. p. 166.

8. C.R. Boxer. *The Dutch Seaborne Empire,* London, 1966, p. 55.See also J. De Vries. *De Economische Achteruitgang der republic in der achttiende eeuw.* Amsterdam. 1959.

9. A. van Dantzig. *Dutch Company Solders and African Politics on the Guinea Coast.* Legon. 1975. Unpublished paper.

10. See W.E.B. Du Bois. The Rape of Africa. In, *The World and Africa.* 10th edition. New York. 1978. p. 57.

11. House of Commons committee report in Ingram. *History of Slavery and Serfdom.* London. 1895. p. 152. Quoted here from W.E.B. Du Bois. Ibid. p. 65.

12. A.C. Carter. *Neutrality or Commitment. The Evolution of Dutch Foreign Policy* 1667-1795. London. 1975. p. 6.

13. G. Williams. *The Expansion of Europe in the 18th Century.* London. 1966. p. 33.

14. G. Williams. Ibid. p. 33.

15. Amo was born near Axim, and was taken to Europe by an employee of the Dutch West India Company. This German an who took him to Europe gave him as a gift to the Duke of Brunswick-Wolfenbuttel, who in turn put him in the care of his son, Augustus Wilhelm. Amo was educated under the patronage of these aristocrats, became a university don and well-known bureaucrat in Germany. He returned to the Gold Coast in 1753 and died in Shama in 1756.

16. G. Lewis. Op. Cit. P. 21. See also S.T. McCloy Negroes and Mulattoes in 18th century France. In *Journal of Negro History.* 30. 1945. pp. 276-292.

17. Estimate by Ziggi Alexander, in Lindsay Mackie. Tapping the deep roots of Britain's Blacks. *The Guardian* London. December 27, 1980.

18. V.G. Kiernan: *The Lords of Human Kind.* London. 1969. p. 195.

19. Quoted here from V.G. Kiernan. Ibid. p. 194.

20. Bosman. Ibid. p. 94.

21. J. Barbot. Ibid. chapter 5.
22. K. Ratelband. (ed.). *Vijf Dagregisters van het Kasteel Sao Jorge da Mina*. The Hague. 1953.
23. P. de Marres. *Beschrijvinghe en de Historische Verhael,can het Gout Koninekrijck van Guinea, anders de Gout Custe de Mina genaemt*. Amsterdam. 1602. (1913 edition). p. 196.
24. See *Zo wijd de Wereld strekt*. Publication from exhibition in honour of 300th anniversary of the death of Johan Maurits van Nassau-Seigen. December 20, 1979. 149 under Johannes Vingboons, *Kasteel Mina en Fort Nassau*. The Dutch Forts on the Gold Coast were St. George d'Elmina, Coenraadsburg-Elmina, Nassau, Moree, Fort Amsterdam, Kormantijn, Leidsaamheijd-Apam, Goede Hoop-Bercoe, Crevoeceur in Accra, Dorothea at Akoda, St Anthony at Axim, Batensteijn at Butri, Fort Hollandia, Fort Witzen at Takoradi, Fort Orange in Sekondi, Fort St Sebastian at Shama, and Vredenburg at Kommany.
25. Bosman. Ibid. p. 99.
26. Bosman. Ibid. p. 100.
27. Harvey Feinberg. *Elmina, Ghana: A History of Its Development and Relationship with the Dutch in the 18th Century*. Unpublished Ph.D. thesis. Boston University. 1969. Chapter 3.
28. Bosman. Ibid. pp. 98-99.
29. See this same text: Chapter on Capitein's life history.
30. See Ibid. chapter on Capitein's life history. A useful study on evangelics of this period is H.W. Debrunner. Sieckentroosters, Predikants and Chaplains: A documentation of the history of Dutch and English Chaplains to Guinea before 1750. *The Bulletin of the Society for African Church History*. Nsukka. 1964.
31. The present author has had occasion to refute this argument. See K.K. Prah: *The Social Background of Coups d'etat*, Amsterdam, 1973, p. 178.
32. Bosman. Ibid. p. 55.
33. Barbot. Op cit. Book 3. chapter 2.
34. H. Feinberg. Op cit. Pp 163-165. See also J.K.J. de Jonge, *De oorsprong van Nederlands Bezittingen op de kust van Guinea*. Den Haag. 1871. pp. 48-49.
35. H. Feinberg. Ibid. pp. 165-166.
36. See J.B. Amissah, *Markt und Handel an der Goldkuste in 16 und 17 Jahrhundert*. Vienna. 1967. Unpublished Ph.D.thesis, p. 69. A more detailed and complete picture of the social structure can be obtained through a reading of the following: J.M. Sarbah. *Fanti Customary Laws*. London, 1897. H. Feinberg. Op cit. Chapter V. J.E. Casely Hayford. *Gold Coast Native Institutions*. London. 1903.J.B. Christensen. *Double Descent Among the Fanti*. New Haven 1954. An interesting and colourful history of Elmina is provided by J.S. Wartemberg. *Sao Jorge d'ElMina; Premier West African Settlement*. Ilfracombe, 1950.
37. See P. de Marees: *Beschryvinghe en de Historische Verhael,can het Gout Koninekrijck van Guinea, anders de Gout Custe de Mina genaemt, Amsterdam*, 1602, Linschoten Vereeniging. 1913.
38. William Smith: *A New Voyage to Guinea*. London. 1967 edition. p. 116.

39. M. Priestley. *West African Trade and Coast Society. London. 1969. p. 15. See footnote 5.*

40. J.M. Sarbah, Jr: *Fanti Customary Laws.* p. 12.

41. On John Conny: See William Smith, op. cit. Also A. van Dantzig. *Who was John Conny of Ahanta.* Unpublished paper 1975. Also K.Y. Daaku, *Trade and Politics on the Gold Coast, 1600 to 1720*, Oxford, 1970. On John Kabes. See also K.Y. Daaku, Ibid. For Thomas Osiat and Abbocon, see M. Priestley. *West African Trade and Coast Society*, London. 1969. On Birempong Kojo see also Priestley, Ibid. Of course, the list of prominent 18th century Gold Coast Caboceers is much longer and a close study of the period is bound to reveal more. Also the sources mentioned here for the list are not exhaustive.

42. Bosman: Ibid. p. 133. Bosman makes a serious mistake in not being able to comprehend lineage structure and aristocracies within the larger compound society. His observations on this matter are careless and unfortunately arrogant. (See Ibid, p. 137).

43. J. Barbot: *A Description of the Coast of South Guinea.* Book 3. Chapter 2. Quoted here from Churchill's Voyages. vol. 5. 1746.

44. Bosman. Ibid. p. 77.

45. Bosman. Ibid. pp. 132-133.

46. H. Feinberg. Op cit. Page 44. The author produces a detailed description of 18th century Elmina life. Bosman's *paan* probably is what is called a *Kente*. 47. William Smith: *A New Voyage to Guinea. 1744.* See 1967 edition. p. 91.

48. C.R. Boxer: *The Portuguese Seaborne Empire.* 1969. pp. 212-213.

49. See Thomas Astley *Voyage and Travels.* 1745. 1968 edition, Vol. 2. London. p. 96. See also Andra a Delcourt. La France et les Etablishments francais an Senegal entre 1712 et 1763. *Ma amoires de l'IFAN.* No. 17. Dakar. 1952. And J.D. Hargreaves. Assimilation in Eighteenth-Century Senegal. *Journal of African History.* Vol VI. No.2. 1965. p. 178.

50. See e.g. J. Barbot. op. cit.

51. C.T. Boxer's Study: *The Portuguese Seaborne Empire* (see page 28), is doubtlessly an informative and scholarly work worth the 40 years the author put into it. However, I strongly disagree with Boxer's doubt about how far the search for gold was an important original motive for Portuguese voyages before 1442 to West Africa. Gold was in fact, the key motive for these voyages since there was a great scarcity in Europe at that time. Other factors were also relevant, but they were secondary to this economic factor. J.W. Blake. *European Beginnings in West Africa.* Imperial Studies Series. Vol. XIV. (Royal Commonwealth Society). Longmans. 1957. Explains that *Mina* "included the whole region where gold could be bartered for in great quantities: it consisted of a littoral belt, about 160 miles in length, mainly on the east side of Cape Three Points but extending as far west as Axem". According to the Portuguese Chronicler Duarte Pacheco,(*Esmeraldo de Situ Orbis, 1498*), Shama which lies between Elmina and Takoradi was the place where the first gold trade was undertaken.

52. The commodities with which the Portuguese acquired the African slaves and gold were largely of foreign origin. Wheat often came from Morocco, the Atlantic islands, and northern Europe. Cloth and textiles were imported from England, Ireland, France and Flanders, though some Portuguese manufactured cloth was also used. Brass utensils and glass beads were imported from Germany, Flanders and Italy, and oyster-shells from the Canaries. Many of the imports from West Africa were likewise re-exported from Portugal. Much Malagueta (pepper) went to Flanders and many of the slaves went to Spain and Italy before the discovery and exploitation of America diverted the slave trade almost wholly to the other side of the Atlantic. What was, perhaps, of most consequence was that a great quantity of the Guinea Gold which entered Lisbon and was there coined into crusados was re-exported to pay for the corn and manufactured goods which Portugal needed. Thus, Portuguese gold of West African origin helped to put Portugal on the currency map of Europe, so to speak. Certain types of gold coins in northern Europe were called *'Portugaloisers'* for centuries, though struck in places like Zwolle and Hamburg. Boxer points out further that during the period of Don Manual I's rule (1496-1521), every year an average of 170,000 *dobras* (Portuguese mint of gold-weight) was exported from the Elmina post alone. In some years the average was higher. (C.R. Boxer, *The Portuguese Seaborne Empire. London. 1969. pp. 29-31)*.

53. The ideological impact of early Portuguese capitalist expansion can be visualized from the fact that on the 24th of July, 1503, barely 21 years after "Holy Mass" had first been celebrated in West Africa, the chief of Elmina, his principal sub-feudatories and others (300), were baptised by the Portuguese Chaplain. After Christianity had been so accepted, they built a bamboo chapel on Santiago Hill opposite the castle. In a very short time there were 1,300 Catholics in Elmina. For a fuller informative study see R.M. Witgren. *Gold Coast Mission History.* Helene Pfann's *A Short History of the Catholic Church in Ghana* (1965) is a good example of cheap neo-colonial historiography. It, however, contains useful information on the subject.

54. J. Barbot. *A Description of the Coasts of South-Guinea.* Book 3. chapter 3. Quoted here from Churchill's Voyages. Vol. 5.

55. K.Y. Daaku. *Trade and Politics on the Gold Coast* (1600-1720). Oxford 1970. p. 48.

56. K.Y. Daaku. Ibid. p. 65.

57. J.D. Fage. *Ghana. A Historical Interpretation.* Madison. 1966. p. 53. The author adds that after this the Akwamu negotiated an alliance with the Dutch under which Akwamu sovereignty was recognized. The Dutch agreed to pay duty on Gold purchased, and also agreed to offer military assistance if Akwamu was attacked.

58. See J.K. Fynn's very informative text. *Asante and its Neighbours.* London. 1971.

Chapter VI

Education, Ideology, Capitein and Others

The Ghanaian cineast Nee Kwate-Owoo in a recent paper, makes some interesting revelations. He informs us that during the inter-war years,

> a film made by Harold Dickinson entitled *A Man of Two Worlds* had an African hero in a part which portrayed him as a 'native' who was well 'educated' in the West, and who was faced with a contradiction between his African tradition and Western civilization. He chose the latter because the former was 'primitive'.[1]

This was supposed to be the realistic choice, and this was what Western imperialists expected of colonized non-westerners. Western civilization was supposedly automatically and always better, it was unimaginable that a colonized man "would persistently wallow in the morass of his primitive culture" or worse still, if given the alternative (i.e. western culture) still choose his non-western view of life. Whoever after being exposed to the West, preferred his indigenous way of life was an incorrigible barbarian, and this, indeed was the attitude of the early biographers of Capitein who spread the stories around that as soon as Capitein got back to Africa, he took to his primitive ways and turned his back on the Christian God, in whose lore he had been steeped during his formative years in Holland.

Some present-day African cultural nationalists would argue that indeed, if Capitein had returned to Africa in body and spirit, into the murky depths of African animist religious traditions, he would have represented much more palpable and meaningful protest than his historical fidelity to idealist western traditions.

Indeed, Bosman gives an interesting description of a near contemporary of Capitein who allegedly did just that. This man, Lewis Hannibal resembled more the distortions of what Capitein became when he returned to Africa, as portrayed in the very early biographies. According to Bosman:

> Here is another Pagan Prince brought over to the Christian Faith, namely, Lewis Hannibal, King of Syria (which he mistakes for Assinee) on the Gold Coast of Africa, who, after being a long time instructed in the Christian Principles, and Baptised by the Bishop of Meaux, the King being his Godfather, received the Sacrament at the Lord's Supper, on the 27th of February, from the Cardinal de Noailles, and offered at the same time a Picture to the Blessed Virgin, to whose Protection he submitted his Territories, having made a Vow at his Return thither, to use his utmost endeavours towards the Conversion of his Subjects. This Moorish Prince departed on the 24th of this Month, in order to embark at Port Lewis, and be Convey'd home by two or three Men of War, under the command of the Chevalier Damon. Thus far runs our above-mentioned Relation. Now, it is my Task to give you a short Account of the Extraction of this pretended King, and to acquaint you with what happened afterwards. Some Years past the French were accustomed to seize all the Negroes that came on board them, and sell them into the West-Indies for Slaves; amongst which happened to be the before said Lewis Hannibal, Christened by the French; but finding him endowed with a more

sprightly Genius than his Country-Men, instead of selling; they brought him to the French Court, where this Imposter pretended to be Son and Heir apparent to the King of Assinee; by which means he so insinuated himself into good Opinion of the Court, that the King made him several very rich Presents, and sent him back to his own Country in the manner above related; but upon his Arrival he returned; and as I am credibly informed, instead of Converting his Subjects to Christianity, is himself returned to Paganism. You may easily guess at the Resentments of the French Court, after being so ridiculously Bubbled by a Negro-Slave: If you consider that by this means they have lost their Aim, which was to get footing on the Gold Coast; and besides that the pious Intention of his most Christian Majesty, to Convert a Heathen Prince, and Establish him on his Throne, were frustrated; the Cardinal de Noailles and the Bishop of Meaux, laboured in vain; And in short, the whole French Court was disappointed of its Expectations[2]

In the search for the civilized native, perhaps less unbendingly nationalistic types, would probably have preferred a Capitein who mixed traditional African forms with western christian content. However, neither one of these two solutions really solves the problem of the man of two worlds. The point is that the positive historical essence of western civilization lies in its materialism. It is the scientific rationalism of materialist philosophy which gives western culture its historical cutting edge in the form of its material technology. Also the qualitative historical maturation of materialist philosophy itself has developed in western society coterminously with the development of the forces and relations of production. It is the scientific method and materialist philosophy translated to suit the specific features of Asia which makes contemporary China, or Japan after the Meiji Restoration, modern Asia.

Most westernized Africans today reject materialism and accept wholeheartedly the whole tradition of western idealism with Christianity being the hall-mark. Throughout the colonial period until this day, the profession of Christianity confers status and commands social respect. The recognition of these facts of social life have become so well understood that for many, the profession of Christianity is only a nominal categorization. Other superficial characteristics of westernization are adopted and cherished. This makes many Africans more pathetically neocolonized types, than the westernized nationalist Africans they would like to be. The irony of this is that, in order to see one's way completely and effectively through the neocolonial ideological fog, one must develop a philosophically antithetical outlook, the only sort of perspective which enables a neocolonized mind to systematically achieve demystification. It is only when this demystification has taken place, that a proper appreciation of the legacy of the West in Africa can be achieved.

Many people today are surprised; others are shocked by the fact that Capitein in the circumstances that he was, wrote a muscular defence of slavery. But actually, it is the almost 250 odd years which separate us from him which makes him look so curiously strange. Today equivalents of Capitein abound and probably even 50 years from now certain positions and opinions held by many present contemporaries would look sadly anachronistic and shameful. History and its interpretation often unfolds in this way. Yesterday's heroes can on second thought become today's villains, although there are many heroes whose glorious memories become even more strengthened by the passage of time. These latter are real 'all-timers'. There are also some among these who initially are viewed as "no-gooders" but who, subsequent generations on closer examination and realization come to venerate; sometimes in very vulgar taste.

Recently, the reputation and historical significance of Kwegyir Aggrey is coming under closer critical scrutiny and reassessment. In the past, he has been "Aggrey of Africa" without any further necessary qualification, and it has been assumed that his historical impact has been all bright and beautiful. Of course, this myth was born and nurtured in the colonial period, and formed in fact, part of the colonial interpretation of African history. Aggrey has definitely been of significance particularly as an educationist, and has in many ways been great inspirational source for many. But also it should be remembered, that Aggrey was an effective instrument of the intentions of Western colonial powers in Africa. He fitted well into the programme and colonial policy for Africa. Agbodeka has written that,

> When he spoke in Kenya, the Missionaries............ said that 'it would be worthwhile for the white people to keep Dr. Aggrey permanently in Kenya to explain the white people to the natives'.

The Governor too felt that,

> he would prefer to have Dr. Aggrey connected with the Kenya Government than a regiment of British soldiers, because his constructive statesmanship in explaining Europeans to natives and natives to Europeans would be more potent than any military force.[3]

Certainly Aggrey had great intellectual and human qualities. He went through his academic training with flying colours. He won a gold medal for English composition, and general scholarship. Apparently he distinguished himself also by being the first in his college to deliver the first Greek oration in the institution. His personality and human qualities were described by the South African D.D.T. Jabavu thus:

> I was privileged to be closely associated with him in part of his travels in my district and thus was enabled to study at first hand his captivating personality and his versatility as a public speaker.

He gave addresses, each of a distinct stamp to suit the occasion, all strictly practical, never nebulous but always to the point. He excelled in the art of concentrating his thought on one specific topic, finally gathering up his argument, getting it home to the hearts and minds of his listeners with Quintilian effect. His method of extempore speech without the slightest note-paper for reference invested his discourse with a genuineness that astonished his audiences, compelling their admiration. Without doubt he has done more than any other visitor I know of, in the brief space of time, to persuade people in our circumstances of the necessities of racial co-operation between white and black.[4]

Indeed very laudable tasks in a century racked and plagued by national, ethnic, racial and regional differences. But where precisely did he stand in terms of his views on these questions. We are informed that when Aggrey was questioned about a practical way out of inter-racial animosities, he replied:

As against Marcus Garvey's hostility, I teach the doctrine of love and work; as against Gandhi's Indian policy of non-cooperation, I proclaim all the time cooperation.[5]

Smith suggests that Aggrey was intellectually close to Booker T. Washington.[6] His views differed fundamentally with W.E.B. Du Bois. The latter had been very critical of the Phelp-Stokes Commission Reports which Aggrey contributed to. Again we are told that around 1926;

Aggrey was plunged into other controversies at this period. Reverberations of the long educational conflict between the Armstrong-Jesse Jones School and the Dubois school reached the Gold Coast from America. *The Gold Coast Leader* published editorial notes setting forth Dubois' criticisms of the Phelps-Stokes Commission Reports. The editor attacked the type of education advocated by Dr Jesse Jones, on the ground that it was intended 'to make the African fit in with the European's scheme of African exploitation and control'. Dubois found in it a defence against black agitation and a desire to substitute white leadership, white teachers and white missionaries for coloured leadership, and an attempt to decry and discredit the educated black man the world over.[7]

In a letter dated August 28th, 1926, Aggrey wrote to his friend and mentor, Dr. Jesse Jones:

I would certainly like to see you this morning and have a long free and frank talk with you. First of all, I want to assure you that I am counteracting the wrong impression being made upon my people by the articles written and commented upon by Dr Dubois and the local editor. I brought here (I am writing this from Cape Coast) the only copies I have of both Reports and told the local editor what is expressed therein. Above these I have told him, and others whom I have met, your heart, and I can assure you they see things differently.[8]

Another Gold Coaster whose historical role has in the past been generally considered to be heroic but who in fact, represented pro-imperialist forces, is George Ekem Ferguson, whom the Germans referred to as the "white black man".[9] Many others like the Senegalese Blaise Diagne, the Katikkiro of Buganda, or Sir Apollo Kagwa, were also definitely instruments of western power in Africa. Till today, many westernized Africans still remain "black skins with white masks" who help directly and indirectly to maintain the neocolonial connection in its economic and ideological forms. As representatives of pro-imperialist interests, they are fundamentally alienated from the aspirations of the African masses.

Philip Quacoe, another 18th century figure, followed Capitein historically, closely on the heels.[10] Some like Holy Johnson[11] lamented the Japanese victory over Russia. This was in 1904, when other contemporary African nationalists had drawn significant historical meaning from the triumph of the Japanese. In contrast to Holy Johnson's position on this event, men like Chilembwe, Sarbah and Casely Hayford had been inspired by the Japanese victory as many others in the then colonial capitalist world of Afro-Asia.

Such radical criticism which appears to be made in one wide sweep bringing down established historical monuments, accepted paragons of excellence and sources of national pride, rubs most people up the wrong way. It is obviously not simply startling, it creates uncertainty in many minds. To others further reflection may show these strictures to be well founded although they may be considered to be in bad taste. One is not denying these historical figures all exceptional qualities, neither are they complete villains. The point here is that they do not all deserve the almost reverential adoration showered on them. Ekem Ferguson was certainly,

> a man of adequate calibre and equipment, and he had an unrivalled knowledge of the resources, customs, predilections and manners of the various peoples of the hinterland of the Gold Coast.[12]

But one must be fully aware of the fact that Ferguson was an active tool in the service of British imperialism in its strife against German imperialism during the period of the high tide of imperialism and the partition of Africa. As Magnus Sampson wrote;

> When the race of Britain, France and Germany for effective occupation of the hinterland began, Mr Ferguson's knowledge was found most useful. After serving on the German Boundary

Commission in 1886, he was sent up-country to hold the border tribes to their allegiance to the British. The King of Atabubu, who had refused to accept British Protection at the beginning of 1889, was persuaded by Mr. Ferguson to sign a treaty of protection on November 21st, 1890, because of a threat of attack by the Ashantis. A Neutral Zone between British and German territory had been agreed upon at the Berlin Conference; neither party was to acquire exclusive influence within the area, but might make treaties with Chiefs with it as to territories outside. During 1893, it having become known to the Government at Accra that German officers were endeavouring to establish relations with some chiefs in this zone, Mr Ferguson was again sent up to counteract their efforts, and on January 25th, 1894, he concluded, on behalf of the British Government, a treaty of friendship with the tribes on the banks of the River Volta, which were not included in Ashanti or the neutral zone.[13]

What is needed is that, a critical but balanced judgement should be employed in our assessment of African history. Seen through the spectacles of the interests of British colonialism in West Africa, Ferguson was certainly very useful and positively significant but we can surely not say the same thing if we examine his contribution from the viewpoint of African freedom and independence. Nkrumah had some useful advice on the whole problem. He once dryly suggested that;

> when the imperialists praise an African leader he is no good for his people, when he is condemned his people should know they have something in him.

It is absurd for African children to be taught to regard their enslavers as heroes. Blacks who accept Piet Hein or

Michiel de Ruyter as heroes deny their own humanity. Certainly until the 1950s, and perhaps later, African secondary school boys and girls were being taught to admire John Hawkins, the pirate adventurer knighted by Elizabeth I, who in his own words kidnapped natives and was granted a coat of arms consisting of an African;

> bound and captive as a token of the new trade he had opened to Englishmen.[14]

It is perhaps more dramatic to present historical examples and data to drive home the point being made, but that does not mean that the problems of cultural imperialism operate only within the framework of the historical discipline. In the other social sciences as Anthropology, Sociology, Psychology or Economics the same problems and manifestations abound and the same principles and contentions stand. What makes the Shona, Zulu, Ndebele, Yoruba or Kikuyu tribes and on the other hand Walloons, Flemish, Basques, Irish, Scottish and English nationalities, if not some spurious colonial notions which regard African nationalities as brutish and primitive, and therefore tribes not nationalities. The tragedy is that Africans continue to describe themselves in these terms. In a recent reaction to H.G. Wells' gloomy vision of the world fifty years from 1931 when Wells advanced his prognostications, Conor Cruise O'Brien wades into the UNESCO theses of recent times about western cultural domination of the Third World.[15] Simply put the theses is that;

> Third World people get their international news and a lot of their entertainment from the capitalist world so they become culturally dominated by the West.

Conor Cruise O'Brien states this argument and goes on to refute it by asserting that,

> I think all that line of argument greatly

underestimates the vitality, versatility, resilience and capacity, both of absorption and rejection, of non-Western cultures. It is, I believe, an inverted form of the more conventional general Western (and leftishly Westernized) tendency to minimise those Third World attitudes which are not much preoccupied with either West or East, but with their home situation, including the close and bitter antagonisms of near neighbours, culturally close, but lethally distinct, within the same frontiers, or across a border; or both. It is a world of multiple ethnocentrisms, including the colossal ethnocentrisms of the two super-powers, which have the capacity to destroy each other and the rest of us.[16]

It is too true for dispute that regionalism, ethnic rivalry and conflict are rife in Africa to take one area of the "Third World." Unfortunately what should be pointed out rather is that Africans are so conscious of these petty regional identities and push such feeling as may derive from them to such ridiculous and lethal proportions that they forget and underestimate the overwhelming and atrophying effects of neocolonialism and its domination of their economic, political, social, and cultural lives. Of course there is resilience and cultural vitality in African societies, but again it should be pointed out that the potentially truly creative groups and social forces are locally controlled and swallowed up by the dominant economic and social groupings whose better minds and cultural orientation is directed towards the metropolitan countries and their former colonial masters.

In the preface to his study of *The History of Education in Ghana*, Graham makes certain very shrewd remarks about the popularly understood meaning of "education" in probably most parts of Africa. Graham writes that,

The word 'education' is used in many parts of Africa to refer to formal instruction in European-type schools. Those Africans who have been to

109

school are said to be 'educated'; all others —
whether they have learnt some trade or not — are
regarded as uneducated.[17]

The truth of Graham's remarks is almost self-evident.
However, few Africans today are self-consciously aware of
these facts, and even fewer understand some of the wider
implications of all this. Thus, the meaning of pre-western
types of socialization processes and mechanisms in African
societies are misunderstood or underestimated in terms of
their social and cultural significance. This ignorance has
been partly bred by the lack or absence of study of education
in "traditional" Africa, and the closely linked lingering idea
that those socialization processes which prevailed before
western contact were activities of primitive and backward
peoples which do not deserve scrutiny or scholarly
examination.[18] The next point in this sort of obscurantist
argument is then that, education and civilization were
introduced by Christian westerners in the course of their
civilizing mission. The cause becomes the consequence. It is
rather glibly assumed that without Christianity there can be
no civilization, no modernization, no technological
development to galvanize Africa into the 20th century. Part
of the reason as J.H. Oldham indicated years ago was that
for a very long time the field of education was left
exclusively to Christian missions.[19]

Actually, the African masses did not automatically or
spontaneously come to these misinformed conclusions. These
ideas were taught by the "colonizing" western interest
groups or groups linked to them, and the early leading
African westernized economic and social classes thrown up
in the wake of western commercial and trading activities
along the coast.[20] Albert Memmi arrives at a similar
conclusion on this issue. He writes that:

It is common knowledge that the ideology of a
governing class is adopted in large measure by the
governed classes. Now, every ideology of combat
includes as an integral part of itself a conception

110

of the adversary. By agreeing to this ideology, the dominated classes practically confirm the role assigned to them. This explains inter alia, the relative stability of societies; oppression is tolerated willy-nilly by the oppressed themselves. In colonial relationships, domination is imposed by people upon people but the pattern remains the same.[21]

In a remarkable book published in 1926, the author blatantly argued that:

In so far as he is Christianized, the negro's savage instincts will be restrained and he will be disposed to acquiesce in white tutelage.[22]

Basically, education in precapitalist African society was an adaptive process for the integration of pre-capitalist man into the contemporary society. It implied training people to respond and fit into existing relations of production, and the internalization of relevant cultural responses to material and non-material pre-capitalist culture. It reflected the interests of the ruling classes by not bearing in its structure and content overt ideological forms antagonistic to the status quo and the existing state. But like all historical entities, it partly bore in itself covertly the seeds of its own historical negation. During the 17th and 18th centuries, indigenous African education was dominated by a feudalist ethos and ideas of deference and submission to aristocratic authority were tempered by the inculcation of sentiments and symbols of ethnic solidarity.

The earliest western educational efforts on the Gold Coast had been Portuguese in origin. King Joao III had instructed his subjects in Elmina to take special care to command that the sons of the Negroes living in the village learn how to read and write, how to sing and pray while ministering in church.

Portuguese educational efforts lasted long. In 1572, the school still existed. Their successors on the African coast, the Dutch established their first educational institution in Elmina in 1644, which reputedly lasted two centuries. Of course, its life must have been spasmodic and truncated. Thus, by the time Capitein came to the Dutch-Elmina teaching scene, a hundred year Dutch tradition in education had been established, however, all available pointers indicate that Capitein's efforts were perhaps the most serious, made under Dutch aegis in the direction of the formal western education of Africans on the Gold Coast during the 18th century. The Danes established their own educational institution in Christiansborg (Osu) in 1722. Between 1737 and 1771 the Moravian Brethren made a number of fruitless attempts to establish a missionary educational foothold. In the British controlled Cape Coast Castle, a missionary, Thomas Thompson, started a school in 1751, which produced Philip Quacoe who, in 1765 continued the missionary and schoolmaster activities of his predecessor. Today Quacoe is well-known and remembered in Ghana but the earlier and in many ways more significant pioneer and certainly more nationally conscious fore-runner Capitein is less known. This is perhaps mainly because during the period of British colonial rule in the Gold Coast, British historical educational efforts in the Gold Coast were played up more prominently than the efforts of the Portuguese, Dutch and Danish. Indeed, it is possible to argue that during particularly the first 200 years of European presence on the Gold Coast, the growth process and fortunes of the various christian denominations which tried to establish footholds in the Gold Coast to a considerable extent depended on the power and influence of the particular European nation principally supporting the particular denomination. Thus, the fortunes of the various denominations reflected the developmental trends in capitalist rivalry on the Gold Coast. In this respect, it is worth noting that for a hundred and fifty years after the Portuguese Catholics had first celebrated Mass on January 12th, 1482, Portuguese Catholic priests as well as Augustinian and Capuchin .Missionary efforts collapsed until the nineteenth century when on the 1st May 1880, the Catholics resumed their evangelical activities on the Gold Coast, again initially in Elmina.[23]

Foster makes an interesting observation about the unique character of the backing christian-educational work enjoyed in the Gold Coast as compared to other parts of Africa. In the greater part of Africa, early western educational efforts were sponsored by European missionary organizations. However, in the case of the Gold Coast, for a whole period in the initial stages these efforts were essentially supported by the merchant companies.[24]

Capitein's educational work is among other things, significant in the sense that generally during the 18th century in the various educational institutions that were attempted on the Gold Coast, the pupils were largely drawn from castle mulattoes. Capitein's Elmina school seems to have been the only one at that stage with a broader selection base.[25]

By attempting to Christianize Africans, apart from motivations of pure religious zeal, the Portuguese and subsequent European powers in Africa were creating African minds which would be openly responsive to religious, but also more importantly non-religious European intentions in Africa.

Education in a wider sense, where and whenever it takes place trains the mind and action to be intelligently active in the world in which we live. It bequeaths the mind with the knowledge and culture of the past in order to make man highly adaptive for the present and be able to meet the future confidently. The executors of this inheritance of culture, the custodians of knowledge, live in the material world, and for their direct and indirect didactic efforts and social contributions, appropriate a share of the material results of production. As non-productive elements in society, they are a sort of parasitic group whose interests are closely linked with the ruling classes. The knowledge they impart is generally in the interest of the ruling classes, and throughout history, they have been known to treat as despicable heretics, radical dissenting types in their own ranks. On the whole, intellectuals have been more conservative than they will care to admit which is to be expected since they belong to the ruling classes or are closely linked to them. Whenever intellectuals have worked for change on behalf of the oppressed masses, they have had to disengage themselves very self-consciously from their class connections both materially and intellectually. The price of this disengagement has been often victimization, isolation, imprisonment or death.

Obviously, many faint-hearted intellectuals die many times before they really die, suffering deaths of the mind before the body. The rigours, woes and tribulations of a revolutionary existence obviously deter many mandarins from adopting radical postures of mind and action, but for most the sheer conditions of class benefits and privileges are the real but unadmitted borders of intellectual pursuits and enquiry.

Many intellectuals are neither faint-hearts nor daredevils, and non-scientific or scientific crusades may lead them to weak and partial probings or challengings of the status quo. In these instances, like Capitein, these challenges may be most often unsystematised, incoherent, and rather muffled protest; sporadic explosions of personality created by inner contradictions and external conflicts which derive from material existence itself. Perhaps Capitein's drinking habits in Elmina and probably the social deviance this implies should be partly seen in conjunction with the frustrations of a man who could not marry the woman he loved. Despite his Dutch education, he was not accepted as equal by his European colleagues although within the hierarchy of the Elmina castle social structure he was second only to the Director-General. The national oppression which he and his kind suffered conflicted with his privileged class position. In the absence of a clear ideology of national resistance, the additional complexities and effects of the limitations imposed by a relatively high class situation, social expression of the frustrations and tensions arising out of these material existential contradictions could be politically, inarticulatedly manifested as growing drinking habits. Capitein died at a youthful age, a curious phenomenon, tormented in and out, financially bankrupt, but with a rich experience of which unfortunately for us, there is precious little known. Capitein was in many ways a more successful pastor of the castle than many of his predecessors or successors. It was very difficult to maintain the moral fibre of the castle crowd, and some of Capitein's successors in letters showed that their work had not been easy. Brill, who in the early 1750s, was appointed pastor, asked the authorities to repatriate him soon after he had arrived. Backering, in a letter dated 13th January, 1756, indicates that he ran into serious difficulties with the Director-General of the castle and was "imprisoned" by the Director-General. Verbeet another pastor, also was involved in bitter conflict and was demoted in terms of his official rank. In all, these conflicts one common factor seems to have been the issue of the sexual morality of the castle community.[26]

Capitein lived in two worlds throughout his life except, perhaps, before he was "stolen" from his parents. Before that time, he was a typical 18th century African infant. The circumstances of his early life are unknown, however, one thing is certain, he must have, as a straddling youngster, had a real attachment to his language until he left for Europe in 1728. It is very doubtful if he ever spoke it while he was there. After he came back 14 years later, remarkably he did the first known translation of "The Lord's Prayer" and other christian doctrinal articles into Fanti.

Soon after he was "stolen" he got into the hands of interests directly representing on the Gold Coast, the Dutch West India Company. From that time until his death his total social role and education was largely controlled by the company's interests or forces close to it. In this world he was a member of a very oppressed nationality but obviously economically much better placed than most of his kind. He was brought up closely in the image of Dutchmen who were directly or indirectly involved with slaving along the West African coast. When he came back to Africa, it was in their employ not as a trader in worldly commodities, rather as one in heavenly ones, although he apparently mixed up these two types of commodities and dealt in both. Capitein's post-1725 life was firmly fitted into the world of early 18th century Dutch seaborne capitalism. He was brought into their social structure first in the forts of the Dutch trading company, later in Holland with clergymen close to the company; and on his return, in the employment of the company. In the circles of the European traders he was economically well looked after but racially regarded and treated as inferior. In the world of Elmina *Krom* (Township) his compatriots regarded him highly, but educationally he had been programmed to work for the immediate interests of the West India Company. In one world (the dominant) economic constraints kept him in orbit, in the other world national factors related him directly to his African compatriots. The dynamics of this situation faced the early 18th century African Capitein very squarely, and he did not have the comfort of age and experience to steel and temper his mental stamina. He was a young man. All this indicates that his modest social and historical achievements were considerable and significant beyond what a superficial contemporary examination of the man may in the first instance suggest.

Perhaps nothing is more telling and indicative of the subtlety and success of 18th century Dutch capitalist ideological interests, shaping and programming Capitein's mind, than his thesis. What had happened was that out of a raw untutored mind of an African slave child, a systematic programme of Western religious education had been fed with such success that as a mature young man with classical Western education, Capitein could present an intellectually argued defence of slavery: That atrocious system which had made his kind the then most degraded humankind. Formed and programmed in this way, he was sent back to his people to carry out cultural propaganda work in the interest of Dutch capitalism. Of course, he was not aware of all this. To him, he had simply been taught the elements of a superior culture, and he was very enthusiastic about enlightening his heathen kind with his knowledge. Many of his mentors must have also entertained false ideas about their ultimate goals and objectives.

Capitein's education indeed became the bonds of his own enslavement. In Europe, he had argued the christian legitimacy of slavery. In Elmina, he must have daily heard the cries of anguish and sorrow of his fellow Africans, held as captive human commodity, in the abominable dungeons of this formidable castle; by the same people who held him often in scorn and ridicule, and for whose purposes he diligently laboured. Whereas, his physically enslaved countrymen often resisted directly and physically the conditions of the cruel oppression they were in, within the confines of the same slave castle, Capitein's possible resistance in his condition of ideological enslavement was expressed perhaps only in the form of extravagant drinking bouts, disputes with his Dutch colleagues, and his unsuccessful commercial activity. Capitein's ideology was anti-revolutionary. It was pitted against the interests of the contemporary labouring classes. It justified socio-economic hierarchy and exploitation, and was cultivated on the dope of Calvinist religious dogma administered within the role of an 18th century missionary to the castle community and the people of Elmina. As a bourgeois African element he was ideologically, of course, more historically progressive than the feudal warlords and chieftains who prosecuted the slave supplying wars, although he was also a beneficiary of the then capitalist slavocracy. For, he was paid by the very Dutch company which bought slaves from the African coast and sold them in the Americas and the West Indies. He was a sort of "compador of religious commodities" who consumed ham and European wines in mid-18th century Elmina.

In this era of neocolonialism and racist rule in Southern Africa, for Africans, the enslavement of Africans in Capitein's time in a way registers as a faint echo of a changing but fundamentally continuous historical phenomena of African exploitation. One difference is important. Whereas, in the 18th century almost all enslaved Africans were physically enslaved, today the bondage is most seriously ideological. In other words, Capitein's own personal type of enslavement has become the dominant contemporary form. It is, of course, often more difficult to recognize, and therefore more difficult to destroy. For overseas Africans ideological and physical oppression has been a particularly long standing affair of untold sorrow and woe. The internment in Elmina (or any such place) was only an early stage of a long chronicle of national oppression from which Africans in diaspora are still not free. Afro-Americans visiting Africa and seeing the interior of these castles are often eaten up by deep sorrow and have their faces drenched in tears, the same way that Jews today visiting Hitler's former concentration camps like Belsen, Dachau, Auschwitz, are moved to tears by the harsh reminder of the sad history of the Jewish people.

There is sufficient evidence to show that Capitein's formal educational and intellectual achievement was well appreciated by his African contemporaries, after all the Ashanti King Opoku Ware was so impressed that he sent 14 Ashanti kids (12 boys and 2 girls) to the then Director-General De Petersen, to be sent to Holland for education, in order to have more Africans as educated as Capitein. The kids ended up on Capitein's Castle School.[27] The Director-General was also satisfied with Capitein's work and he wrote favourably on Capitein's work to the *Bewindhebberen* in Holland. Capitein's knowledge of Akan (Fanti) was very useful to the castle and Elmina community of the period. In some of the transactions with the Grandees and Caboceers Capitein featured as interpreter. The Dutch authorities could not have had a better interpreter.[28] In Elmina, Capitein continued his own theological studies. In a letter of De Petersen to the *Bewindhebberen* dated 15th February, 1743, the Director-General wrote that he had handed the following books to Capitein, which the latter had requested some time before — (1) *Acta Synodalia*; (2) *Salomon Van Til, Voorhow der Heydenen*; (3) *Eusebii, Praeparatio et demostratio evangelica*; (4) *Spanhemii, dubia Evangelica*; (5) *Weshovii, In Passionem*; (6) *Poli-Synopsis*; (7) *Rabbi David Kimchius, vel R. Salomon Jarchi, In Vestus Testamentum*; (8) *Opera Ainsworth*. As Eekhof rightly indicates these titles indicate the direction and area of Capitein's intellectual preoccupation during this period of his life.[29]

Capitein apparently did his best to sustain his castle school but little enthusiasm for his educational activities was shown by the W.I.C. employees, and as time went on weak attendance and poor support for his efforts continued to undermine his work. At one point in the early months of 1743, in an effort to increase the number of his pupils, Capitein went as far as arguing out to the Grandees that as subjects of the Dutch authorities in Elmina, they were obliged "without further delay" to bring their children to the castle school. The Grandees agreed to do this and also promised to bring other children to the school. As a result, at a point there were 45 pupils in the school.[30] It was one of Capitein's unrealized plans to render the Akan language into a structured written form, although in his own overmodest words, he doubted if the language "was in all respects expressible".

In the 18th century Gold Coast Capitein must have been a famous figure, and it is rather unfortunate that the conspiracy of circumstances prevented his work from having long lasting effects. In present day Elmina, very little is known about Capitein, and unfortunately oral tradition is extremely thin on Capitein.

Apart from a number of places in South Africa, particularly in the region of the Cape, there is probably nowhere else in Africa where the Dutch left such historically indelible marks of their presence in Africa as Elmina. Dutch derived words appear in the vocabulary of the Akan people. *Doek* (a piece of cloth) has become *Duku* in Akan. *Brood* (bread) is *Brodo* in Akan. The place abounds with Dutch names, descendants of the Dutch colonists of the 17th, 18th and 19th centuries. They include names like Petersen, Haick, Bartels, Van Hein, De Heer, Des Bordes, Vroom, Van Kijk, Scheck, Van der Puije, and others. One comes across Dutch street names such as *Buitenrust*. The town has an old Dutch cemetery dating from the early 19th century. Today it is one of the exotic monuments in the town. Dutch-type architecture is not uncommon although today these buildings like most others in Elmina are seriously dilapidated.

Apart from the wretched state of houses in present-day Elmina, this old historic town is today horrifying in its poverty and the way poverty has reduced its inhabitants to atrociously squalid and dehumanizing conditions of existence. The town reeks with a sickening stench, there is a near absence of any form of sanitation. All this gives a deeply saddening impression when it is remembered that this very town had been the first real western town on the Gold Coast, a town which more than any other served as a bridgehead for the establishment of western society in Guinea. This was the first point where western ideas made a safe landing. Capitein died and was most probably buried in Elmina, although his grave is unknown.[31]

Like the old city, the famous castle is today falling into decay. The chapel in which Capitein performed his religious ceremonies is today together with the rest of the castle falling into ruin. Lawrence estimates that it was constructed around 1662.[32] It has an impressive facade and a set of rather imposing rounded windows. Above the main doorway of the chapel is written "ZION IS DES HEEREN RUSTE DIT IS SYNWOONPLAETS IN EEUWIGHEY" — (Psalm 132) (Zion is the Lord's rest, it is his dwelling place to eternity).

Notes

CHAPTER VI

1. Kwate Nee-Owoo. *Notes on the Colonial Cinema*. Mimeograph. London, 1975.
2. William Bosman. *Description of Guinea*. pp. 420-421. London. 1967.
3. F. Agbodeka. *Achimota in the National Setting*. Forthcoming book. chapter 2.
4. E.W. Smith. *Aggrey of Africa.*, *pp. 165-166.*
5. Ibid. p. 124.
6. Ibid. p. 121.
7. Ibid. p. 255.
8. Ibid. p. 256.
9. See Magnus Sampson. *Makers of Modern Ghana*. Vol. I. p. 91. 1969 edition.
10. Philip Quacoe was born in 1741, son of a well-known Cape Coast Caboceer Birempon Kodzo. He was sent to Britain in 1754 together with 2 other youngsters, on the commendation of the missionary Thomas Thompson under the auspices of the Society for the Propagation of the Gospel. Quacoe's two companions died in Britain. Quacoe was trained and ordained as a minister of the Church and appointed: "Missionary, Catechist and Schoolmaster to the Negroes on the Gold Coast in Africa with a salary of 50 Pounds per annum with effect from 25th March, 1765". Quacoe was back in 1766, and in the same year started a school for mulatto kids. Quacoe initiated an Educational Society called *The Torridzonian Society* in 1787. Quacoe had considerable success with his school, and died in 1816. For a fuller account see F.L. Bartels. Philip Quacoe 1741-1816. In, *Transactions of the Gold Coast and Togoland Historical Society*. Vol. I. Part V. 1955.
11. See E.A. Ayandele: *Holy Johnson.* (*James Johnson: Pioneer of African Nationalism 1836-1917*). London. 1970. p. 193.
12. Magnus J. Sampson. Ekem Ferguson of Anomabu. *Transactions of the Gold Coast and Togoland Historical Society*. Vol. II. Part 1. Achimota. 1956. p 41.
13. Magnus J. Sampson. Ibid. p 37.
14. W.E.B. Du Bois. The Rape of Africa. *In The World and Africa*. New York. 10th Printing. 1978. p 51. Du Bois' source is C. Cohen. Christianity, Slavery and Labour. London. 1931. pp. 46-47.
15. See *The Observer* (British Weekly of which C.C. O'Brien was Editor-in-Chief). 28th December, 1980.
16. Ibid.
17. C.K. Graham: *The History of Education in Ghana*. London. 1971. (See his preface, first paragraph).
18. Among notable recent exceptions can be mentioned. Helen Callaway. Indigenous Education in Yoruba Society .F.L. Bartels. Akan Indigenous Education.T.J.L. Forde. Indigenous Education in Sierra Leone.N.K. Dzobo. Values in Indigenous African Education. All these articles appear in G.N. Brown and M Hiskett (ed). *Conflict and Harmony in Education in Tropical Africa*. London. 1975. Of course, other material on the subject of indigenous education exist, but by and large the subject has to date been

rather poorly researched.

19. J.H. Oldham. *Christianity and the Race Problem*. London. 1924. p. 105.
20. See my *Essays on African Society and History*. Accra 1976. Particularly. pp. 12-13.
21. A. Memmi. *The Colonizer and the Colonized*. London. 1965. p. 88. Translated from the French. *Portrait du Colonisé a precedé du Portrait du Colonisateur. 1957.*
22. Lothrop Stoddard. *The Rising Tide of Color*. London. 1926. pp. 96-97.
23. The material for this last paragraph is drawn from two main sources: (a) P. Foster. *Education and Social Change in Ghana*, London. 1967 edition. chapter 2. (b) Helene Pfann. *A Short History of the Catholic Church in Ghana.* Cape Coast. 1965. Part I.
24. P. Foster. *Education and Social Change in Ghana*. 1967. p. 44.
25. See P. Foster. *Education and Social Change in Ghana*. London. 1967. p. 45.
26. This information was collected by my friend, Simon Simonse from various Dutch Archives.
27. See Eekhof. Ibid. p. 56.
28. Eekhof. Ibid. p. 51.
29. Eekhof. Ibid. p. 48.
30. Eekhof. Ibid. p. 50.
31. The present author has undertaken his own fruitless search for the grave.
32. A.W. Lawrence. *Trade Castles and Forts of West Africa*, London. 1969. p. 143.

SKOTAVILLE BIOGRAPHIC SERIES

MAKEBA, MY STORY:
Miriam Makeba with David Hall

The most inspiring book I have read, packed with feeling. Emotions of love, hate, sadness and pride over what Miriam has achieved tear you apart at the same time. — *Maud Motanyane*.

ISBN 0 947009 39 6

LEST WE FORGET:
Philip Ata Kgosana

It was Kgosana who made headlines when he led thousands of anti-pass demonstrators in Cape Town on March 30, 1960, shoving aside his university studies. The inevitable exile followed after both the PAC and ANC were banned; exile either in foreign lands or in South African jails. Here is a poignant account of a man and his times, re-enacting for us the drama of those turbulent days. It is an authentic voice, for he was right there in the frontline. —*Es'kia Mphahlele*.

ISBN 0 947009 42 6

HIGHER THAN HOPE:
Fatima Meer

This is an extraordinary account of Nelson Rolihlahla Mandela and his times. It covers the most significant period of the ANC, and the most formative two decades of the existing turmoil in South African politics.

It is an affectionate gift for Rolihlahla on his 70th birthday.

ISBN 0 947009 59 0

An investigation into Zanu's strategies

ALSO FROM SKOTAVILLE

IZWI LABASEBENZI

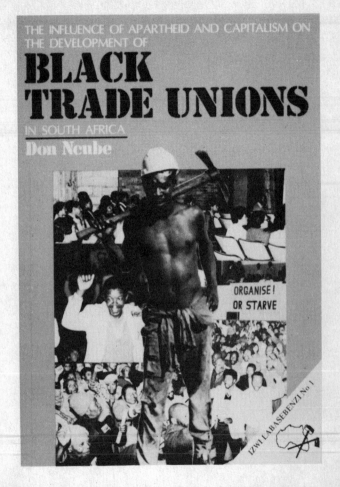

This book analyses the historical birth, demise and re-emergence of Black unions in South Africa; it covers the spectrum of general, industrial and co-ordinating union bodies. These emerged as vehicles to ameliorate the appalling conditions to which Black workers were subjected; and to serve as countervailing forces to oppose the existing oppressive power imbalance.